Vol 1
Ten Bible-based sessions for your 14 to 18 youth group

Copyright © Scripture Union 2008
Reprinted 2009
ISBN 978 1 84427 358 4
Scripture Union, 207–209 Queensway, Bletchley, MK2 2EB, England.
Email: info@scriptureunion.org.uk
Website: www.scriptureunion.org.uk

Scripture Union Australia, Locked Bag 2, Central Coast Business Centre,
NSW 2252 Australia
Website: www.scriptureunion.org.au

Scripture Union USA, PO Box 987, Valley Forge, PA 19482, USA
Website: www.scriptureunion.org

Scripture quotations taken from The New Century Version
(Anglicised edition) © 1993 by Nelson Word Ltd, 501 Nelson Place,
PO Box 141000, Nashville, TN, 37214–1000, USA.

British Library Cataloguing-in-Data
A catalogue for this book is available from the British Library.

Cover and text layout design by Martin Lore
Internal layout by Creative Pages, www.creativepages.co.uk
Written by Phil Green, Darren Hill, Geoff Harley-Mason
Edited by Phil Green, Darren Hill, Helen Jones
Printed and bound in Singapore by Tien Wah Press

Scripture Union is an international Christian charity working with churches
in more than 130 countries, providing resources to bring the good news about
Jesus to children, young people and families and encouraging them to develop
spiritually through the Bible and prayer.

__Welcome

From the Editor

Welcome to SUbstance! A new and fresh youth group resource for 14 to 18-year-olds.

This, the first volume, contains two crucial modules that will provide an essential foundation to your young people's faith. The first provides an overview of the biblical story as we focus in on six key scenes. It aims to help your group connect God's story to their lives, as, after all, God's story is not finished yet!

The second aims to equip them as they develop their faith. As we explore the Bible, prayer, worship and church they'll hopefully discover how dynamic and life-changing a relationship with God should be.

As we continue to develop SUbstance we would love to hear from you. So, please contact us and tell us about what you love, what you don't love and how you think we could improve this resource.

We hope that SUbstance will inspire both you and the young people you work with. Enjoy!

Phil

__Contents

In this volume...

Foundation Prime Module

Spirituality One Module

__How to...

...use SUbstance

Everyone knows that no two groups of young people are the same. SUbstance has been developed with that point in mind. Each session contains a variety of ideas for large groups and small ones, groups that meet in large halls and ones that meet in small sitting rooms, groups that are desperate to explore the Bible, and groups that, more often than not, are somewhat disinterested.

The ideas in this leaders' guide can be used and adapted, or completely ignored! But hopefully, this highly adaptable and easy-to-use resource will help you create gripping sessions that will get your group stuck into the Bible. These sessions aim to encourage and challenge, engage and equip, allow for times of quiet reflection, loud debate and laughter, and provide in-depth Bible study that is both soul searching and practical.

Does this sound like what you've been looking for? Can't wait to get going? That's great! But, before you do, just take a few minutes to read the instructions. In order to make the sessions highly adaptable and flexible to suit the needs of your group, this leaders' guide follows a simple framework. This is what each session includes:

Aim: So you know where the session is heading. All the ideas in the session seek to work towards the aim.

Introduction: This contains some background information for you. It will prepare you for the session ahead by introducing you to the topic, highlighting any particular issues and providing a little biblical background.

Begin: A choice of 'icebreaker' type activities that aim to introduce the theme, set the tone of the session, and make the group feel relaxed with one another.

Explore: A variety of ways of engaging with the session's aim and key Bible passage(s). The type of approach taken varies between sessions. However, there is usually a 'lighter' idea, one that 'delves deeper', either in terms of bible study or application and then one more 'creative' idea. One idea is usually accompanied by a Journal Page (see below).

Respond: A selection of ideas to help young people respond to what has been explored. This section includes prayer, praise, reflection and practical ideas along with opportunities to discuss how the learning should be applied.

Journal Page: Each session has a photocopiable page for group members. These are designed for groups that want to 'delve deep'; they include background material (usually taken from the leader's introduction) and are normally related to one of the ideas in the 'Explore' section.

There are usually three ideas in each of the sections, but occasionally a fourth idea will sneak it's way in – at no extra cost to you! The suggestion is that you choose one idea from each section to make up your session. However, depending on the time and resources you have available, you make like to use more of the ideas. All the ideas are designed to 'stand alone'; however some of them naturally build on from each other.

There is also a whole range of additional resources for you to use to make the sessions even more memorable and effective. They can be downloaded from **www.scriptureunion.org.uk/substance**. They include video presentations, quizzes, images, animations, fact files and PowerPoint presentations. Still excited? Well, it's now time to get stuck in!

__How to...

...ask good questions

There are plenty of opportunities in SUbstance sessions for group discussion. Asking good questions is the key to facilitating discussion. Through asking good questions you can open up the discussion or focus on a particular issue and you can guide and prompt the conversations. Good questions will enable the young people to learn from each other as they explore what the Bible has to say.

Here are a few helpful hints when it comes to asking good questions.

Ask open questions, not closed questions

Closed questions are questions that can be answered with one word and they rarely create discussion. (Questions that can be answered 'yes' or 'no' are closed questions). Open questions, as the name suggests, open up opportunities for discussion. An example of a closed question would be, 'Did you enjoy the session last week?' An example of an open question would be, 'What did you enjoy about the session last week?'

When necessary ask 'sub questions'

For example, if you are asking your group to discuss ways that they can practically love other people it might be helpful to ask sub-questions such as 'How can we show our school friends love?', 'How can we show our families love?', and 'How can we show the people we really don't like love?'

Is there a point to the question?

For example, if you are looking at a Bible passage and you ask questions such as 'How many different animals are mentioned in this passage?' it is unlikely to create any discussion, and why ask that question anyway – what's the point of it? Make sure you know what you are trying to achieve by asking a particular question, and before you ask it, think through how the group may respond.

Rephrase the question

If people don't understand the question you are asking them it can help if you are able to rephrase it. By simply putting the question another way, perhaps by changing the emphasis slightly, you can help someone else understand it. For example, 'What is the meaning of life?' is a very difficult question to answer. However, if instead you begin the discussion by asking, 'What sort of things give life meaning?' you are more likely to get a response and start a good discussion.

Give examples

Another good way to help people understand the question is to give examples. This allows them to see the 'type' of response you're expecting and this should give the young people confidence to say what they are thinking and therefore kick-start the discussion. Once the discussion has started the responses will probably begin to broaden.

Hopefully, some of these hints will help. But remember, the more you know the group, the easier it will be to ask appropriate questions that will get the discussion rolling. Therefore, make sure you invest time in getting to know the young people in the group, and also make sure you allow plenty of time for them to get to know each other. Discussing issues with friends is always easier (and more enjoyable!) than discussing issues with strangers.

Essential Kit List

You'll always need to have the following items to hand. Anything else you need will be listed at the beginning of the idea.

Bibles
Large sheets of paper (e.g. flip chart)
Marker Pens
A4 Paper
Pens and Pencils

Foundation

God's story is an amazing story. It's a story that spans eternity; therefore, it's quite long and can sometimes be rather difficult to get our heads around! This module aims to provide an overview of God's story by focusing on six key scenes. As we delve into God's story we'll learn so much about God, his plans, and how we are significant characters in the story.

Creation

Aim__To explore how holding the belief that God created the heavens and the earth impacts on how we live our lives.

__Leaders' Introduction

The first verse of the Bible says, *'In the beginning God created the sky and the earth.'* Whether or not you accept this statement to be true will affect EVERYTHING else.

There is a lot of debate amongst Christians surrounding creation. Did God create the world in six, literal, 24-hour days? Does the big bang or evolution explain how God created the universe? Should we read the first chapters of Genesis literally or more like a poem? The aim of this session is NOT to get caught up in these discussions. Rather it is to communicate that Christians believe that God made the universe and he made us for a reason. Believing that God made us, and we are not here just by chance, should radically change the way we view the world and our lives. It enables us to live our lives with a sense of purpose.

Genesis 1:26–30 says a lot about our purpose. Verses 26 and 27 speak of how we are 'made in the image of God'. This phrase is quoted a great deal, and rightly so – it's extremely significant. However, there may be a lot more to it than people often think.

The writer of the book of Genesis probably didn't come up with the phrase 'made in the image of God' by himself; it's likely that he 'borrowed' it from someone else. It is now thought that the book of Genesis was written during the Israelites' exile. During that period the kings of Babylon were often described as being 'the image of the gods'.

Therefore, in saying humans are 'made in the image of God', the writer of Genesis is saying, 'The Babylon kings think that they are the image of the gods, but you are made in the image of the one true God, the creator and king of the entire universe'. However, with the label 'image of God' comes responsibility as well as value.

In order for any Babylonian king to be 'an image of the gods', they had to act as a representative for the gods here on earth. They were responsible for making sure the world was taken care of and everyone got on well with one another. The same is true when it comes to us being 'made in the image of God'. We are his representatives on earth, and with that comes responsibility as Genesis 1:26–30 explains to us.

There are three things that we must learn from this when it comes to our purpose.

- **A relationship with God.** We can't represent someone we don't know; therefore we need to have a relationship with him if we are going to be his representatives.

- **Relationship with other people.** God didn't design us to live in isolation. Genesis 2:18 tells us that it is not good for us to be alone. Just as the Babylonian kings were expected to help people live in harmony with one other, God expects us to help others – it's a message that is repeated many times throughout the Bible. It follows that if we are God's representatives on earth, we should treat people like God would treat them. For example, if someone feels down we should listen to them, help them and maybe give them a hug – because I'm sure that's what God would do if he was physically here right now. Jesus provides us with the perfect model of how we are meant to represent God to others.

- **Look after creation.** We are not just to take care of other people; we have a responsibility for all that God has made (Genesis 1:26–30).

__Begin

Idea 1

__Title: Made by...
__Why: To introduce the idea that everything is designed and made
__With: Resource page 71 and 72 and maybe a prize

> Page 72 contains twenty inventions. Page 71 contains twenty inventors. Photocopy both pages (ideally onto different colours of card) and cut out the names.

> Divide the group into a few small teams, give each team a complete set of 'invention' cards and 'inventor' cards and ask them to match up the invention with their inventor. Give a prize to the winning team.

> Conclude this section by using the following illustration:
Isaac Newton once built a very detailed model of the solar system. One day a friend of his, who was an atheist came to see him and asked him who had made the model. Newton told him that nobody had made the model. His friend complained, saying that it was ridiculous to say that nobody had made the model. Newton responded by saying that if he thought that this model needed a maker how much more does the actual universe require a maker? Complicated things, such as watches, aeroplanes and computers don't just appear or design themselves; they need a designer and maker. The universe is so complex surely it had to be designed and made?

Idea 2

__Title: What is it?
__Why: To see that things are made for a reason
__With: A selection of bizarre objects (or pictures of) and maybe a prize

> Either bring in a variety of bizarre objects or *download* photographs of bizarre objects from **www.scriptureunion.org.uk/ substance**.

> See if the group can guess what they are. You could do this as a competition.

> Conclude this activity by explaining how all these objects, however bizarre they might appear, were all made for a reason. To find out what it's for, you may well have to ask the person who designed it. And, if you don't use the object for the right reason, you are likely to damage it. (You may well remember that when CD-ROM drives first appeared in computers, on more than one occasion helplines received phone calls from people complaining that their computer's coffee cup holder had broken!)

Idea 3

__Title: Amazing facts
__Why: To be blown away about how amazing God's creation is
__With: Resource page 73, video presentation and means to display it

> Divide the group into small teams and use the quiz on page 73. It's a true or false quiz based around some amazing facts about our planet and the wider universe.

> At the end of the quiz pose the following question to the group, 'Is it really likely that such an amazing universe happened by chance? Surely it had to be designed and made?'

> *Download* the video presentation from **www. scriptureunion.org.uk/substance** and show it to your group. This presentation includes some amazing pictures of creation along with some more mind-blowing facts.

__Explore

Idea 1

__Title: First things first
__Why: To explore how belief in a creator God changes everything

> Read Genesis 1:1 and explain how whether or not you believe this verse to be true affects everything else in your life.

> Divide the group into two (if your group is large you may want to divide into four or more groups instead). Ask one group to discuss how someone would view life if they thought that God created the world and ask the other group to discuss how someone would view life if they did not believe God created the world. Give them a large sheet of paper and pens to make notes on and encourage them to consider questions such as:

___What is the value of your life?
___What's the purpose of your life?
___How do you decide what's right and wrong?
___Is there more to life than the 'material' world we see around us?
___Is there any ultimate authority? If so, what's it like?
___What happens when you die?

> Once they have discussed this for a while ask each group to summarise their discussion to the other group(s). Then as a whole group discuss the advantages and disadvantages of each approach to life.

Idea 2

__Title: It was good
__Why: To celebrate how good God's creation is
__With: That depends!

> Use some of the following ideas to celebrate how good God's creation is. You might want to set up different 'stations' around the room.

> Read Genesis 1:1 – 2:3. This could be done creatively by getting the group to act it out, rewrite it in their own words, turn it into a song or poem or record a news bulletin about it.

> Listen to Rob Lacey's account of creation. (*The essential word on the street* – Track 1)

> If you didn't use the video presentation as a 'begin' activity you could use it as part of this section. (You can *download* the video presentation from **www.scriptureunion.org.uk/ substance**).

> Get artistic. Provide your group with paints, clay or play dough and ask them to draw or make something they want to thank God for.

> A–Z of creation. In groups ask the young people to come up with a list from A–Z of things in creation they want to thank God for.

> Have three large sheets of paper, write one of the following questions on each and get the young people to write or draw their thoughts.

___From the creation account what can we learn about God?
___Why do you think God created so much variety?
___What do we learn about ourselves and the purpose of life?

Idea 3

__Title: Created for a purpose
__Why: To explore what the purpose of our existence is
__With: Journal page

> The aim of this section is to communicate what the purpose of life is – in terms of being made in the image of God. If you didn't use idea 1, you may like to begin this section by asking the group to discuss the question: 'If we are here by chance (ie we were not made by God) what is the purpose of life?'

> Divide the young people into small groups and ask them to read and discuss Genesis 1:26–30 using the questions on the journal pages. What can we learn about the purpose of life from these verses? What does it mean to be made in the image of God? How does being made in the image of God make you feel? After they have had enough time to work through the journal page give each group an opportunity to feed back their thoughts and questions with the wider group.

> Prepare a short talk using the information provided in the leader's introduction. You may like to begin with the following story to illustrate how significant purpose is.

In concentration camps during the Second World War one of the tasks the captives were sometimes asked to do was dig a massive hole and move the soil to the other side of the field. Sometimes they would do this for an entire week. Then, just when they thought they had finished this exhausting work, the guards would tell them to move all the soil back and fill up the hole they had just dug. Captives in concentration camps had to do all kinds of hard labour and unbearable tasks, but apparently this was one of the worst. That's because it lacked any point; there was no purpose to it whatsoever. Life devoid of purpose is very hard to cope with.

> How can we ensure that we are living our lives in a way that reflects the image of God? (Jesus is the best example we have as to what it means to reflect the image of God.)

> If God was physically on earth right now what would he be doing? What would his priorities be? Therefore what should we be doing, and what should our priorities be?

__Respond

Idea 1

__Title: Praise God
__Why: To praise and give thanks to God for his amazing creation
__With: Depends on exactly what you decide to do!

> After thinking about how amazing God's creation is why not finish the session by spending some time praising God? You may like to use some of the ideas from Idea 2 of the 'Explore' section and/or some of the following ideas.
> Listen to or sing some of these songs (links to the lyrics can be found on **www.scriptureunion. org.uk/substance**):
___He Reigns – *Newsboys*
___Let Everything that has Breath – *Matt Redman*
___For the Beauty of the Earth – *Folliot S. Pierpoint*
___Creation's King – *Paul Baloche and Graham Kendrick*

> On a massive sheet of paper write, draw or paint things you want to thank God for. After a while encourage people to pray individually (or in pairs) thanking God for the things that appear on the paper.
> Go for a walk and while you walk thank God for the things you see around you.
> Get people to surf the Internet and produce a PowerPoint presentation, ideally set to music, which celebrates how good God's creation is.
> Encourage people to write a song, poem or rap that praises God for his amazing creation.

Idea 2

__Title: We have a responsibility
__Why: To explore what we can do to take care of the planet
__With: Photocopies of page 74

> We are all very aware that the environment is struggling to cope with the pressure humans are putting on it – pollution, global warming, animals becoming extinct – the list could go on. You may like to begin this section by giving your group some statistics (you can *download* some from **www.scriptureunion.org.uk/ substance**); however, this may not be necessary, as your group are probably only too aware of the problems.
> If Internet access is a possibility you could get the young people to find some videos on the Internet that communicate the importance of caring for the planet. While the group are searching the Internet (or as an alternative) encourage them to discuss these questions:
___What are some of the environmental problems facing the world?
___Why should we be playing our part in making a difference?
___Why can it be hard to motivate ourselves to do something about the problems? What should we do about this?

> Give everyone a photocopy of page 74 and, in conversation with each other, get them to work through their 'typical' day, coming up with ideas of how they can make a difference.

> You can *download* a sample day, along with some interesting statistics, from **www.scriptureunion.org.uk/ substance**.

Idea 3

__Title: Job description
__Why: To get people to think about what they want to do with their lives
__With: Small pieces of card

> Depending on what ideas you have used during this session, it is likely that you've spent quite a bit of time considering the purpose of life. Therefore, why not conclude the session by getting everyone to write a 'Job description' for their life?
> Begin by explaining how when you apply for a new job you will receive a 'Job description' which outlines the main responsibilities you'll be expected to undertake. Perhaps you could download a few sample job descriptions from the Internet.
> Divide the group into twos or threes and encourage them to discuss what they might include in their 'Job descriptions'. As well as getting ideas from the creation narrative you could also suggest they look at the following passages: Deuteronomy 11:1, Ecclesiastes 12:13, Matthew 22:36–40 and Matthew 28:18–20.
> Give everyone a small piece of card and a pen and get them to write down a 'Job description' for their life. Get them to put it somewhere where they'll see it regularly. For example, in their wallet or on their mirror.

> Ask the group to think about how they can help each other achieve what they have written in their 'Job descriptions'. Get them to discuss this in their twos and threes before talking about it as a whole group. Conclude by encouraging them to pray for one another.

__Journal Journal Journal

What does the phrase 'made in the image of God' mean?

Well, it probably means a lot more than you think it does!

The writer of the book of Genesis probably didn't come up with the phrase 'made in the image of God' by himself; it's likely that he 'borrowed' it from someone else. It is now thought that the book of Genesis was written during the Israelites' exile. During that period the kings of Babylon were often described as being 'the image of the gods'.

Therefore, in saying humans are made in 'the image of God', the writer of Genesis is saying, 'The Babylon kings think that they are the image of the gods, but you are made in the image of the one true God, the creator and king of the entire universe'. However, with the label 'image of God' comes responsibility as well as value.

In order for any Babylonian king to be 'an image of the gods', they had to act as a representative for the gods here on earth. They were responsible for making sure the world was taken care of and everyone got on well with one another. The same is true when it comes to us being made in 'the image of God'. We are his representatives on earth, and with that comes responsibility as Genesis 1:26–30 explains to us.

There are three things that we must learn from this when it comes to our purpose.

- **A relationship with God.** We can't represent someone we don't know; therefore we need to have a relationship with him if we are going to be His representatives.

- **Relationship with other people.** God didn't design us to live in isolation, Genesis 2:18 tells us that it is not good for us to be alone. Just as the Babylonian kings were expected to help people live in harmony with one other, God **expects** us to help others – it's a message that is repeated many times throughout the Bible. It follows that if **we are** God's representatives on earth, we should treat people like God would treat them. For example, if someone feels down we should listen to them, help them, and maybe give them a hug – because I'm sure that's what God would do if he was physically here right now. Jesus provides us with the perfect model of how we are meant to represent God to others.

- **Look after creation.** We are not just to take care of other people, we have a responsibility for all that God has made (Genesis 1:26–30).

Read Genesis 1:26–30. How does it make you feel about yourself?

What can we learn about the purpose of life from these verses?

What do you think it means to be made in the image of God?

How can we ensure that we are living our lives in a way that reflects the image of God?
[Think about Jesus – he's the best example we have as to what it means to reflect the image of God.]

If God was physically on earth right now what would he be doing? What would his priorities be? Therefore what should we be doing, and what should our priorities be?

Living with purpose

The purpose of my life is...

Questions, thoughts and doodles

Fall

Aim__To explore the consequences of living in a fallen world.

__Leaders' Introduction

In this session we will be exploring what is often known as 'the fall narrative'. The account in Genesis 3 explains how sin entered the world and the serious consequences this had.

Sin: it's nasty and it's not something that many of us want to talk about. In fact we'd quite like to brush it under the carpet. It is great looking at what the Bible has to say about how much God loves us and how fantastic Jesus is. However, talking about sin, looking at how messed-up the world is, and indeed our own lives are, is never such an attractive proposition. But, it has to be done! You might ask, 'Why?' Well...

Firstly, it explains the mess we find ourselves in. In the previous session we explored how good God's creation is. But you only have to watch the news for a few minutes or flick through a newspaper to see how so much of what we see around us cannot be described as good. The fall explains what went wrong and therefore helps us make sense of what's going on in the world today.

Secondly, if we don't grasp the bad news we will never realise why Jesus is such good news. Many people ask the question, 'Why is Jesus good news?' We might respond, 'Because he saves us from our sins.' To which many people might reply, 'Well, I don't need Jesus then, because I'm not that bad – I don't need saving.' In my experience many people, especially young people, believe in some form of God and in some kind of afterlife. However, many of these people don't think they need Jesus, because they reckon that they will be OK. They believe that when they die God will let them into heaven because they have never done anything that bad. They think that hell is only for the 'really bad people', for those people who have committed serious crimes, like murder and rape. However, that's not the message of the Bible. The fall, and the consequences of the fall, makes it very clear that we are all sinners and that we all need Jesus. Therefore, we need to talk about sin

(appropriately), because if we don't grasp the bad news we won't realise why we need to take Jesus seriously.

So, talking about sin is essential – it might not be the most fun session you'll ever have, but that doesn't mean you can miss it out!

This session will provide you with an opportunity to explore the fall narrative with your group. As you do this, you'll learn vital lessons about God and human nature. You'll be able to consider why Adam and Eve sinned, discover the consequences and be blown away by God's amazing response. Whatever you do, make sure this session isn't just about studying a narrative; make sure the words jump off the page into our present-day lives. We can learn so much about God, the world we live in and ourselves from this passage.

There is a lot of bad news in this session; however, it doesn't need to be all doom and gloom – hope should filter right through your time together. Once we grasp how serious sin is, and when we realise that despite our sin God still loves us and is desperate to have a relationship with us, we should be even more amazed at how awesome God is!

__Begin

Idea 1

__Title: What happened next?
__Why: A fun way to introduce the idea that after creation something went wrong
__With: Downloaded video clips, laptop, video projector, speakers (if necessary) and maybe a prize

> *Download* the series of 'What happened next?' clips from **www.scriptureunion.org.uk/substance**. Show the first half of the clip, then press pause and get the group to guess what they think happened next. Then play the remainder of the clip. This could either be done as a competition or just for fun.
> Introduce the session by explaining how last time we were exploring how God created the world and it was good. However, when we look around us today we see that it's certainly not all good. In this session we will consider what happened next – what did go wrong?

Idea 2

__Title: So much bad news
__Why: To consider the consequences of the fall
__With: Newspapers, big paper, glue and scissors

> Introduce this activity by recapping the last session: *In Session 1 we looked at how God created the heavens and the earth and how it was all good. However, it doesn't take you long to discover that something must have gone wrong, because so much of what we see in the world today cannot be described as good, instead we would have to say it's bad.*
> Divide the group into threes or fours. Give each small group a few newspapers along with some scissors, glue and a big sheet of paper. Ask them to produce a collage illustrating the mess the world is in and how much bad news there is.
> Alternatively **download** and watch the 'What went wrong?' video presentation from **www.scriptureunion.org.uk/substance**.
> Once your group has either created a collage or watched the video presentation, ask them to imagine they are aliens that have been sent to earth on a recognisance mission. The aliens have heard that this species called 'humans' have got themselves into a mess and they are keen to learn from their mistakes. These questions might help the group get started:
___What sort of problems do humans face?
___Why are human beings and their world in such a mess?
___What might this say about them?
___What might this say about their maker?

> Let the discussion run fairly freely. Make sure their ideas are written down and then refer to them throughout the rest of the session.

Idea 3

__Title: Is God not doing his job?
__Why: To consider who's to blame for the mess the world is in
__With: *Bruce Almighty* DVD and the means to show it

> Watch a clip from the film *Bruce Almighty* (rating 12). Start watching it at 00:17:12 (Bruce is about it get into his car when he notices a group of men picking on a homeless person) and stop it at 00:22:15 (when Bruce's pager starts beeping, soon after he's shouted, *'The only one around here who is not doing his job is you…answer me!'*)
> During this clip Bruce blames God for the problems he's experiencing in his life. He doesn't simply feel ignored by God; he thinks God is picking on him. *'God is a mean kid sitting on an anthill with a magnifying glass and I'm the ant. He could fix my life in five minutes if he wanted to, but he'd rather burn one of my feelers and watch me squirm.'*
> Introduce the clip by explaining that Bruce has just lost his job. Once you have watched the clip, divide the group into twos or threes and encourage the young people to discuss how they might respond to Bruce. If you would like to explore the issues in more depth some of these questions may help:
___What evidence is there to suggest that God is not doing his job?
___Why do some people feel like God is ignoring them or picking on them?
___Why do some people blame God for the mess the world is in?
___Do you think it's his fault? Why (not)?
___What evidence is there to suggest that God is still doing his job?

> Conclude this section by making a list of some of the problems the world is experiencing at the moment. Don't just think about the big, global scale problems (eg global warming and war), but also think about the problems people experience at home, school and in their local communities. Then discuss which of these problems human beings are responsible for. Explain that in this session we will be looking at how the problems facing the world are our fault, not God's.

__Explore

Idea 1

__Title: 'Disaster Strikes!' news report
__Why: To creatively explore what went wrong
__With: That depends on how ambitious you are!

> Explain to the group that they are reporters and they have to present an engaging account of what went wrong after creation.
> Divide the young people into small groups and get them to create news reports based on the account of the fall found in Genesis 3. You can be as creative with this as your time, resources and nerves allow! For example, you could get the groups to record it for radio using sound-recording equipment or they could prepare a story for a television news bulletin which they could film before showing to the rest of the group. (Make sure you check out what your Church's Child Protection policy has to say about filming young people before you undertake this activity.)
> Encourage them to make use of interviews. You may also like to give them some of the following pointers:
___What was life like for the various characters before and after the fall?
___How do the characters feel about what's happened?
___What exactly went wrong and who's to blame?
___Why did things go so horribly wrong?

Idea 2

__Title: Learning from the fall
__Why: To explore what we can learn from the fall narrative
__With: Journal page 19

> Put some dramatic, maybe classical, music on in the background. Ask the group to sit comfortably and close their eyes. As you read Genesis 3 to the group, ask them to reflect on what we can discover about God, the devil and humankind from this passage. Once you have read the fall narrative to them encourage them to spend a few moments continuing to reflect on what they've just heard.
> Divide the young people into small groups to discuss their thoughts and to work through the journal page.
> Alternatively, you may want to facilitate a whole-group discussion. If so, some of the following questions may be helpful. Don't try to use them all! Just use a question, when necessary, to prompt and guide the discussion.

God rules, but the devil is at work
___Why does the devil want people to disobey God?
___Read what the serpent says in Genesis 3:1. Was this really what God had said? (Read Genesis 2:16–17 to check.)
___It appears that the devil twisted God's words. Why do you think he did this?
___In what ways are people today influenced or tempted to disobey God?
___When it comes to life and the enjoyment of it, why should we listen to God rather than the devil? What evidence is there that God wants us to enjoy life?

We want to be 'God' (verse 5)
___When we disobey God, what are we 'saying' to him?
___Why do people want to be 'God'/King/in charge of their own lives?
___Why does this cause so many problems?

Our choices matter (verse 6)
___Were Adam and Eve forced to eat the fruit?
___Why did they choose to?
___Why do you think God made us with the ability to make choices? What can we learn about God from this?
___What would life be like if you couldn't make your own choices?
___Why do people choose to disobey God? Why is it sensible to obey God?

God's response (verse 8,9)
___If someone hurts you, what would be your initial response?
___What was God's initial response to Adam and Eve?
___Why do you think God didn't just give up on us? What can we learn about God from this?
___How does this make you feel?
___What should our response be?

Idea 3

__Title: Consequences
__Why: To learn that Adam and Eve's actions have consequences – as do ours
__With: Possible PowerPoint presentation and the means to display it

Get your groups to discuss some of the possible consequences for these actions:
___Helping your parents clean the house.
___Smoking.
___Buying someone a present.
___Stealing a CD from a shop.
___Bullying someone at school.
___Eating too much food.

You may like to **download** the accompanying PowerPoint presentation from **www. scriptureunion.org.uk/ substance**.
> If you haven't used ideas 1 or 2 you'll need to provide a brief overview of Genesis 3:1–6. Then divide the young people into twos and threes before reading and discussing the following:
Adam and Eve's sin had consequences. Read Genesis 3:7–10.
___What were the initial consequences of their sin?
___When we do things wrong, why might we want to hide it from other people?
___When we do things wrong, why might we want to hide from God?

Read Genesis 3:11–24.
___What were the other consequences of Adam and Eve's sin?
___Which of these consequences are still obvious in the world today?

> Conclude this section by summarising the consequences of sin. (See journal page)

__Respond

Idea 1

__Title: Ashamed?
__Why: To reflect on the shame caused by sin and point to Jesus
__With: An appropriate song and the means to play it

> In the fall narrative we read of Adam and Eve hiding from each other and God – they undoubtedly felt a whole range of emotions including shame, guilt and regret.
Get hold of one of the following songs (or perhaps you know of a more appropriate one) and get your group to reflect on what has been explored in this session. You may like to have the lyrics available for them to read as the song is playing.
__Fix You – Cold Play
__Let it fade – Jeremy Camp
__Without you – Lonestar
__Shame – Depeche Mode

> Once the song has finished, leave a few minutes of silence before explaining that even in the bleakness of Genesis 3 there is a glimmer of hope. In verse 15, as God rebukes the snake he says, 'One of her descendants will crush your head,' which is a reference to Jesus. Because of Jesus we can come to God without shame. He will take away our guilt and help us deal with our regrets.
> Have a time of prayer. You may like to simply encourage the young people to say their own prayers to God in the quiet, you might encourage a few people to say prayers out loud, or you might decide to ask one of the leaders to say a prayer on behalf of the group.
> This session may well raise issues for some of your group. Therefore, make sure there are leaders available at the end of the session for young people to chat to if they would like to.

Idea 2

__Title: Let God be God
__Why: To encourage young people to let God be God

> In the fall narrative we read how the snake tempted Eve to eat the fruit by saying that if she did, she would 'be like God'. When we sin, we are saying to God that we don't want to follow him; we want to go our own way. We don't want him to be in charge of our lives, we want to be in charge. We don't want him to be God; we want to be 'God' of our own lives.
> Undertake the following activity either individually or corporately (if your group is large you may want to divide into a few small groups).
> **Individually**. Get everyone to draw a very quick sketch of themselves in the middle of a sheet of A4 paper – a stick person will be more than adequate! Then all over the paper ask them to write and/or draw as many things as possible that make up their lives – family, friends, activities, hobbies, passions, dreams and ambitions – everything! After they have done this, encourage everyone to prayerfully consider which of these things they are allowing God to be in charge of, or which ones they 'want to be God' for and shut God out.
Encourage them to chat about this in twos or threes and then pray for one another.
> **Corporately**. Get one of your group to lie on a big sheet of paper and draw round them. Then ask everyone to write and/or draw as many things around the outline of the person that make up their lives. After this has been done, ask everyone to think, and discuss in twos or threes, about which of these things they are allowing God to be in charge of, or which ones they 'want to be God' for and shut God out. Conclude by praying for one another.

Idea 3

__Title: Influence, decisions and consequences
__Why: To consider what things influence the decisions we make and what the possible consequences of our decisions are

> During this session we've discovered how Adam and Eve were influenced to eat the fruit, that God made humans with the ability to make their own decisions, and that the decisions we make have consequences. Undertake this exercise with your group:
> Give everyone a sheet of paper and get them to divide it into three columns.
> Title the SECOND column 'Decisions' and write down a selection of decisions we have to make.
> Title the THIRD column 'Consequences' and write down the various consequences of each of the decisions we make.
> Mark each of the consequences to show whether they are positive (+) or negative (–).
> Indicate which consequences were short-term and which ones were longer-term (set a scale between 1 and 5, 1 being short term and 5 being long term.)
> Title the FIRST column 'Influences' and write down what might influence each of the decisions. Underline the biggest influences. Think specifically about how as Christians we should go about making decisions.

> This idea will hopefully provide a framework for an interesting discussion.

God rules, but the devil is at work

God rules, but the devil is certainly active and has influence. He wants to do anything he can to interfere with God's plans. The devil hates it when people follow God, so he does whatever he can to stop them.

We want to be 'God'

When we sin we are saying to God that we don't want to follow him; we want to go our own way. We don't want him to be in charge of our lives; we want to be in charge. We don't want him to be God; we want to be 'God' of our own lives.

Our choices matter

God could have created us as robots; he could have created us in such a way that we had to obey him. But he didn't. He wanted to be able to have a real relationship with us, and you can't have a real relationship with a robot. A real, meaningful relationship with God is only possible if we have the ability to make real choices. However, choices have consequences.

God's response

God's initial response was to come looking for Adam and Eve in the garden and ask, 'Where are you?' Humans sin and God comes looking for them. That's what so much of the Bible is about. Humans turn their backs on God, but God doesn't turn his back on us. Humans ignore God, but God tries to get their attention.

Consequences

The fall had consequences; so do our sins.

1) God designed us and he knows what works best. By disobeying him we mess up our own lives and the lives of those around us.
2) God is a perfect and holy God. The sin we commit separates us from God making a relationship with him impossible.
3) Without a relationship with God we will not be able to spend eternity with him in heaven.
4) The fall affected the whole of God's creation causing 'weeds and thistles' (Genesis 3:18) and natural disasters (Romans 8:20–22).

While reading Genesis 3 reflect on what we can discover about...

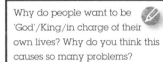 ...God

...the devil

...humankind

Why do you think the devil wants people to disobey God?

When it comes to life and the enjoyment of it, why should we listen to God rather than the devil? What evidence is there that God wants us to enjoy life?

Why do people want to be 'God'/King/in charge of their own lives? Why do you think this causes so many problems?

Why do you think God made us with the ability to make choices? What would life be like if you couldn't make your own choices?

Why do people choose to disobey God? Why is it sensible to obey God?

If someone hurts you, what would be your initial response? What was God's initial response to Adam and Eve?

Why do you think God didn't just give up on us?

What were the initial consequences of Adam and Eve's sin?

What consequences of sin can we see around us today?

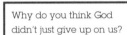 Questions, thoughts and doodles

Exodus

Aim__To see that being a people of God demands holy living.

__Leaders' Introduction

Creation was good, very good, but then people made a bit of a mess of things. Well, that's a bit of an understatement – they made a massive mess of things! As the story of God and the people he created advances, we continue to read about lots of people making lots of mistakes, but God does not give up on his people. As we read through the book of Genesis and move onto Exodus we begin to realise that God has a plan! It's a plan to reveal himself to the world and make it possible for people to relate to him. It begins with Abraham and continues as Jacob and his sons end up in Egypt, then many years later Moses leads God's people out of Egypt towards the Promised Land (the land which God promised Abraham and which the Israelites have been longing and waiting for). It is here that a nation really begins to take shape – a nation that God desires to live under his rule and to reveal him to the entire world.

In this session we are going to catch up with Moses and the Israelites just before they make their final entry into the Promised Land. God has led them out of Egypt with an incredible display of his power. But along the way, instead of remembering how faithful God has been, the people frequently doubt him, turn away from him and even begin worshiping other gods. God is not pleased with their behaviour and as a result they have to wait another 40 years before being able to actually enter the Promised Land.

In this session we will be looking at some passages from the book of Deuteronomy which are accounts of what is, in effect, Moses' final briefing to his people before the final push into Canaan. Deuteronomy is a book that reveals so much to us about what God is like and how he wants his people to live.

The name Deuteronomy literally means Second Law. This does not mean that it is either an additional or different law from the one given to Moses on Mount Sinai. Deuteronomy provides us with a faithful and more detailed version of the original. On the brink of moving to their Promised Land, Moses gives the people more details on the meaning and application of the Law along with a motivational talk about the way ahead. It's all about preparing them to build a new nation. They are to build a nation that is different from the other nations. They are to be a nation led by God, a people who follow God's way.

Moses warns the people what it is going to be like and tells them of some of the challenges. He warns them in chapter 6 of three things: not to forget the Lord (verse 12); not to follow other gods (verse 14) and not to test or doubt that God is who he says he is (verse 16). These warnings are there because Moses knew it would be easy for the Israelites to do them. The same warnings are very relevant for us today, aren't they?

A major theme running through Deuteronomy is the importance of passing truths on to the next generation. It's therefore a very interesting and encouraging book for anyone desperate to see young people learning about the ways of God. Try to set aside some time before you lead this session to read the whole book (or at least read the first six chapters). As you do this, why not mark the times that Moses mentioned children or the next generation? Let's remind ourselves what a privilege and responsibility it is to work with young people.

__Begin

Idea 1

__Title: Final pep talk
__Why: To begin to consider Deuteronomy as a motivational talk
__With: A copy of the film *Crimson Tide* and means to show it

> In *Crimson Tide* Captain Frank Ramsey (Gene Hackman) takes his submarine, the USS Alabama to the Pacific Ocean to defend the USA from a potential nuclear missile strike from some dissident Russian rebels. Show the scene where Captain Ramsay speaks to his crew in the pouring rain giving them their final pep talk before going off into action. One of his motivational lines is, 'I expect and demand your very best. Anything less, you should have joined the air force!' (00:14:22 – 00:17:00)

> Having watched the clip, get the group to discuss what they thought of the Captain's talk. You may want to divide the young people into smaller groups. Encourage them to consider the following questions:

___How well did it motivate his crew?
___Was it effective in preparing them for the mission ahead?
___In that situation would you have done anything differently?

> If you are unable to get hold of a copy of *Crimson Tide* there are many other films that include motivational speeches. In fact, you may know of one which you think will work much better with your group.

Idea 2

__Title: A post-nuclear community
__Why: To understand that communities need rules

> Paint the picture of a futuristic time when the world has suffered from a nuclear war. There is a remnant of people who have survived by locking themselves in a radiation-proof bunker for many years. It is now safe to re-emerge into the world where they need to set up a new community and rebuild the human race.

> The group consists of 12 people – 7 men and 5 women. (Alternatively, depending on the size of your group, you could create a scenario that is much more comparable to your group!) Some have managed to bring belongings with them, while others have nothing. One person in the group lost both their hands in the war. You may choose to give your group more 'details' about what the people in the group are like!

> Divide the young people into smaller groups and ask each group to create a set of ten rules for this new community. They must be simple and easy to understand and must help the group as they seek to rebuild the human race.

> Once each group has decided on their ten rules get them to tell everyone why they have chosen the rules they have.

Idea 3

__Title: Don't forget it
__Why: To realise that it's important to remember God's laws
__With: Maybe a prize

> Divide the group into small teams and give each team a piece of paper and a pen. Get each team to write down as many different ways they can think of for remembering things. (For example, writing it on your hand, setting an alarm or tying a knot in a handkerchief.) After a few minutes get the teams to read out their lists and give them points. If no one else thought of a particular method on their list give them two points, if another team wrote down that method as well just give them one point.

> You may also want to play some other memory games. For example:

___In teams get them to memorise the order of an entire deck of playing cards.
___Put about 20 small objects on a tray. Get the young people to look at them for about 30 seconds. Then take the tray away, remove an item, and see which team can shout out what the missing item is first.

__Explore

Idea 1

__Title: Motivated
__Why: To explore Moses'
motivational speech as a
group
__With: Music and the means to
play it, maybe bean bags and
big cushions

> Using the information
provided in the Leaders'
Introduction explain to the group
the journey the Israelites have
been on. Now, you are about to
look in on Moses as he gives
his last briefing to the Israelites
before they make their final move
into the Promised Land.
> There are two extremely
different options as to how you
could approach what happens
next! One option is chilled and
reflective, the other is high-
energy, but either option should
get the young people thinking
about the same issues.
> **Option 1**: Get everyone to
make themselves comfortable.
Bean bags or cushions would be
ideal. Play some gentle music in
the background and encourage
people NOT to fall asleep!
Explain to the group that you are
about to read them Moses' final
briefing and motivational talk
before they entered the Promised
Land. As you read Deuteronomy
6 encourage them to think about
the following questions:
___How do you think the Israelites
would have felt as they heard
Moses speech?
___In a few weeks', months' or
years' time, what would be
the main points from this
speech that the people should
remember?

> **Option 2**: Instead of getting
everyone feeling chilled, get
everyone hyped up! Pretend you
are in a changing room about
to go out onto the pitch before a
big sporting contest. Play some
loud up-beat music (for example,
Eye of the Tiger) and do whatever
else sports teams might do
before a big match! Explain to
the group that you are about to
read them Moses' final briefing
and motivational talk before they
entered the Promised Land. As
you read it, in a loud, exciting
and hyped up manner, encourage
them to think about the same two
questions.
> The key to a motivational talk
is, unsurprisingly, motivating
people! Motivation is so important
in order to get anything done!
To study for an exam, to go to
the gym, or to save money all
require motivation. ***Download***
the motivation images from
**www.scriptureunion.org.uk/
substance**. Print the images onto
card and display them around
the room with a sheet of plain
paper next to them. Ask the young
people to go and write down
what might motivate the people
to do what the images show.
Encourage them to come up
with both humorous and serious
responses!
> Deuteronomy 6:20–25 provides
a good summary as to what
should motivate the Israelites to
listen to, and follow God. Reread
these verses and discuss with
the group why the Israelites
should have been motivated to
live life God's way. Conclude
by discussing why we should
be motivated to live life God's
way. Depending on the size of
your group (you could always

divide into smaller groups), go
around the group as many times
as possible, encouraging each
young person to give a different
response as to why the Israelites
and we should be motivated to
live life God's way.

Idea 2

__Title: Do's and Don'ts
__Why: To explore how
important and helpful God's
rules are
__With: Journal page 3

> If you haven't already read
Deuteronomy 6 with your group
and explained the context, do so
now. It's quite a long passage
so encourage as many young
people as possible to read a
few verses each. Then, using the
journal page, ask them to list
all the things the Israelites are
commanded to do and all the
things they are commanded not
to do!
> Explain to the group that God
doesn't give rules in order to
constrain us and spoil our lives,
but to enable us to live more
enjoyable and fulfilled lives.
If you used the 'Post-nuclear
community' idea, talk about
how that activity illustrated how
essential rules are. Alternatively,
use a sporting illustration. For
example, a game of football
is much more enjoyable for
everyone if the rules are adhered
to.
> Conclude by exploring the
three warnings (do not forget the
Lord, do not follow other Gods,
do not test the Lord) in more
detail using the journal page that
accompanies this session.

Idea 3

__Title: Animated Motivation
__Why: To enable people
to simply engage with
Deuteronomy 6
__With: Animation file and the
means to show it

> *Download* the animation
file from **www.scriptureunion.
org.uk/substance**. This gives a
concise, easy to grasp overview of
Deuteronomy 6 and its context.
> Once you have shown the group
the animation, divide them into twos
or threes and get them to imagine
they are news reporters. They have
just heard the speech and are about
to have the opportunity to interview
Moses and a member of the
audience. Get them to make a note
of the questions they would ask.
> Once they have come up with
a few questions get them to swap
their questions with another
group. Now they have to imagine
how Moses and the member
of the audience may have
responded to the questions asked
by the other group!
> Gather everyone together and
ask the young people to feed
back the questions and possible
responses.
> Conclude by encouraging
them to discuss the following
questions in their small groups:
___What do you think are the
key things Moses wanted the
Israelites to learn?
___What can we learn about what
it means to follow God from
Moses' speech?
___What should have motivated
the Israelites to follow God?
___What should motivate us to
follow God?

__Respond

Idea 1

__Title: DIY Motivational
   Speeches
__Why: A (hopefully!) fun way
   to summarise the session's
   learning
__With: Video recording
   equipment

> Get everyone (or in twos or three) to create a motivational speech of their own. Then film them presenting it. Make sure you think through the Child Protection issues of filming young people, and everything that takes place in this session adheres with your church's Child Protection policy.
> Before they start give the group a clear brief. Explain that they are to create a motivational speech which would encourage people their own age to live their lives in a way that is distinct and pleasing to God. Explain why they should want to do this and what this would look like in practice.

Idea 2

__Title: Remembering
__Why: It's important to
   remember what God wants
   from us

> It's clear that Moses did not want the Israelites to forget God's Law. This is something the Israelites needed to remember, continue to learn and put into practice. Read Deuteronomy 6:6–9.
> Explain to the group that there appears to be three 'groups' of ways of remembering God's

commandments. If you are interested in finding out more about how Jews go about doing this *download* the factsheet from **www.scriptureunion.org.uk/substance**.

   ___**Family (and Friends) Ways** – 'Teach them to your children, and talk about them when you sit at home and walk along the road, when you lie down and when you get up.' (verse 7)
   ___**Personal Ways** – 'Write them down and tie them to your hands as a sign. Tie them on your forehead to remind you.' (verse 8)
   ___**Public Ways** – 'and write them on your doors and gates.' (verse 8)

> Get the group to make a list of some of the key things they think God would want them to remember. Then ask the group to consider ways (based on the three 'groups' mentioned above) they could do this in the 21st Century. Encourage them to put some of them into practice.

Idea 3

__Title: God is good
__Why: To motivate us to live
   holy lives as a response to
   God's goodness
__With: Worship music and the
   means to play it, and Post-it
   notes

> During this session we've seen that God wanted the Israelites to live holy lives. He didn't want them to do this to spoil their fun or because he was cruel. The opposite is in fact true. God wanted them to obey him

because he loves them so much and wants what's best for them.
> Why not conclude this session by celebrating and reflecting on God's goodness? This is surely the best way to motivate us to follow him and live holy lives.
> Play some worship songs which speak of God's greatness and all he has done for us. While the music is playing encourage young people to write 'Post-it note prayers' thanking God for his goodness. Allow the group to write as many prayers as they would like to. Get everyone to stick all the prayers to a wall, and hopefully, by the end, the wall will be covered with prayers praising God for his goodness.
> As the young people leave the session, encourage them to pause as they walk out and read some of the 'Post-it note prayers'. As they do this ask them to think, 'God is so good and because of that this week I'm going to...' Encourage them to think about how they are going to respond to God's goodness this week.

Journal
__Journal
Journal
Journal

Journal
Journal

Creation was good, very good, but then people made a bit of a mess of things. Well, that's a bit of an understatement – they made a massive mess of things! As the story of God and the people he created advances, we continue to read about lots of people making lots of mistakes, but God does not give up on his people. As we read through the book of Genesis and move onto Exodus we begin to realise that God has a plan! It's a plan to reveal himself to the world and make it possible for people to relate to him. It begins with Abraham and continues as Jacob and his sons end up in Egypt, then many years later Moses leads God's people out of Egypt towards the Promised Land (the land which God promised Abraham and which the Israelites have been longing and waiting for) It is here that a nation really begins to take shape – a nation that God desires to live under his rule and to reveal him to the entire world.

In this session we are catching up with Moses and the Israelites just before they make their final entry into the Promised Land. God has led them out of Egypt with an incredible display of his power. But along the way, instead of remembering how faithful God has been, the people frequently doubt him, turn away from him and even begin worshiping other gods. God is not pleased with their behaviour and as a result they have to wait another 40 years before being able to actually enter the Promised Land.

Deuteronomy 6 is, in effect, Moses' final briefing to his people before the final push into Canaan. Deuteronomy is a book that reveals so much to us about what God is like and how he wants his people to live.

On the brink of moving to their Promised Land, Moses gives the people more details on the meaning and application of the Law along with a motivational talk about the way ahead. It's all about preparing them to build a new nation. They are to build a nation that is different from the other nations. They are to be a nation led by God, a people who follow God's way.

While reading Deuteronomy, make a list of all the things that the Israelites are commanded to do and all the things they are commanded not to do.

Do's	Don'ts

Why are rules so important?

Do not forget the Lord (verse 12)

What did this mean for the Israelites?	What might this mean for us today?

Do not worship other Gods (verse 14)

What did this mean for the Israelites?	What might this mean for us today?

Do not test the Lord your God (verse 16)

What did this mean for the Israelites?	What might this mean for us today?

Questions, thoughts and doodles

Exile

Aim__To learn from the events leading up to the exile.

__Leaders' Introduction

There's a recurring theme throughout the Old Testament – it could be summed up by the phrase 'forwards and backwards'. The Israelites would obey God, things would go well for them and they would move forwards. Then they would begin to forget about God, they'd stop obeying him, sometimes they would even begin worshipping other gods, things wouldn't go well for them and they would go backwards. But God would remain faithful, and eventually they would turn back to God (usually after God had delivered them from an enemy), they'd follow him again and once again they'd move forwards. But then, guess what? They'd begin to ignore God again and they would start going backwards once more. It's a cycle that repeats itself throughout the Old Testament. It's one that may well resonate with you and the young people you work with. You attend a festival and you come back on fire for God, but before long you get distracted and you begin to drift. Then you go to a conference and once again you come back on fire, but it's not long before you begin to slip again.

From the time the Israelites left Egypt until they reached the Promised Land, this 'forwards and backwards' cycle is all too evident. However, in the last session we looked at Moses' motivational speech that explained how they were to be a holy nation, set aside for God. Perhaps now they would get it right? But they didn't. The cycle continued. When the Israelites were going backwards God would provide a 'judge' to get them moving forwards again, but before long they would slip backwards. Then the Israelites wanted to be like the other nations and have their own king. (Before then they were happy for God to be their ruler.) They had good kings that would take them forwards, and bad kings that would take them backwards. Eventually civil war broke out and the Israelites were divided into a northern nation (Israel) and a southern nation (Judah). The 'forwards and backwards' cycle continued. When they were going backwards God would send prophets to urge them to turn back to God. However, as time went on, the prophets were increasingly ignored. Eventually both the northern and southern nations were destroyed and the few remaining Israelites were taken off into exile. It all looked rather bleak. But a remnant remained faithful to God and God continued to work through them. Within a few generations those in exile got to go home and they began rebuilding Jerusalem. They looked forward to the day that the promised Messiah would come.

In this session we will take a look at some of the events leading up to the exile and consider this 'forwards and backwards' cycle that the Israelites got caught up in. But our focus will be on the prophet Jeremiah and a clear warning that he gave the Israelites. Obey God, or face the consequences. In Jeremiah 7 he explains that obedience to God is much more than just 'doing the rituals' – it's about putting God first, doing the right things in the right way and living lives that please God.

Make sure that this session isn't just a history lesson. Take every opportunity to connect the experiences and mistakes of the Israelites to our lives today. There's so much we can learn from them as we seek to live our lives for God.

__Begin

Idea 1

__Title: Forwards and
backwards
__Why: A fun way to introduce
this recurring Old Testament
theme
__With: A fair amount of space
and some statements

> You'll need a fair amount of
space for this activity! Everyone in
your group will need to be able to
stand side-by-side. They will need
to be able to take about three
steps backwards and about ten
steps forwards.
> Say a statement (for example,
'All those who support Manchester
United'). All those people who
support Manchester United can
take one step forwards, all those
who don't have to take one step
backwards. Keep doing this until
someone crosses the finish line!
Here are some more example
statements to get you started:
___All those wearing white
trainers.
___All those who go to X High
School.
___All those who wear glasses or
contact lenses.
___All those who have been in
France.
___All those who have been to the
cinema in the last month.

> Conclude this activity by
explaining that a recurring
theme in the Old Testament is the
people of Israel going forwards
and backwards.

Idea 2

__Title: What matters most?
__Why: To consider what God
wants from us

> Divide the group into twos
and give each pair a piece of
paper and a pen. Ask them to
imagine they are on the bus or
having lunch at school when
someone begins talking to them
about Christianity. They ask the
question, 'What are the most
important things we need to do to
please God?'
> Ask every pair to make a list of
what they consider are the three
most important things we need
to do to please God. Encourage
them to find Bible references to
support their ideas.
> Once they have had time to
do this, gather the group back
together and compare their
lists. Hopefully this will create
some discussion. Conclude by
explaining that in this session
we'll see how the Israelites often
missed the point when it came to
pleasing God.

Idea 3

__Title: Not listening
__Why: To illustrate how easily
we can be distracted and not
listen to God
__With: A lot of distractions!

> Set up the room you meet
in so it's full of distractions.
For example, have some loud
music playing, an episode of
The Simpsons showing on the
TV in one corner and perhaps a
PlayStation set up in the other

corner, a selection of magazines,
some board games and lots of
nice food and drink. Encourage
everyone, including the leaders,
to get stuck into all these
activities as they arrive.
> After a little while, try to start
the session, or at least try to do
the notices! It will probably be
very difficult to get their attention.
After a while, move through to
another room (if possible) or clear
away the distractions.
> Then discuss some of the
following questions:
___What distracts you from doing
homework?
___What distracts you from
watching your favourite TV
programme?
___What distracts you from
household chores?
___What distracts you from
eating?
___What distracts you from
listening to God?

> Conclude by explaining how
throughout the Old Testament
we read how God sent many
prophets to speak to the Israelites
on his behalf, but all too often
they just didn't listen.

__Explore

Idea 1

__Title: Historians
__Why: To explore the events leading up to the exile
__With: Resource page 75 and other resources from www.scriptureunion.org.uk/substance, marker pens and a flip chart

> Divide the young people into groups of threes and explain that they are historians trying to establish what happened to the Israelites leading up to the exile. Using the following resources get them to prepare a short presentation that they can show to the rest of the group. Encourage them to get into the 'mood' and suggest they present their findings in a style of a history lecture or TV documentary.

___Resource page 75
___Video interviews (*Download* from www.scriptureunion.org.uk/substance)
___Newspaper articles (*Download* from www.scriptureunion.org.uk/substance)
___Any books you may be able to find

> After each group has presented their findings, spend some time discussing what we can learn from the mistakes the Israelites made. Do this with the aid of some marker pens and flipchart or large sheets of paper!

Idea 2

__Title: Snakes and Ladders
__Why: To provide an overview of the Old Testament story leading up to the exile
__With: Snakes and ladders board, counters, dice and pens

> This idea could potentially provide you with a structure for the whole session, as it includes a 'begin' activity, an 'explore' activity and a 'respond' activity!
> *Download* the Snakes and Ladders board from www.scriptureunion.org.uk/substance and find some counters and dice. Get everyone in the group playing Snakes and Ladders. The fewer people playing on each set the less time this will take up!
> Explain that throughout the Old Testament, leading up to the exile, the Israelites were continually going forwards and backwards. Divide the group into threes and fours and give each group at least one Bible, a blank Snakes and Ladders template (you can *download* this from www.scriptureunion.org.uk/substance) and a pen. Using the Bible verses below, get them to create a Snakes and Ladders board which explains why the Israelites kept going forwards and backwards. (A sample of this activity can also be *downloaded* from www.scriptureunion.org.uk/substance.)

_ Judges 2:7
_ Judges 2:10–14
_ Judges 4:23–24
_ Judges 6:1
_ 1 Kings 2:1–4
_ 1 Kings 15:25,26
_ 2 Kings 23:25
_ 2 Kings 24:19,20

> Using the leaders' introductory notes prepare a short talk explaining what happened before, during and after the exile. Then get the group to discuss what the Israelites may have learnt though their exile experience.
> Conclude this activity by giving each group another blank Snakes and Ladders template. This time create a Snakes and Ladders board that explains what might cause us to go forwards and backwards in our relationship with God.

Idea 3

__Title: Last warning
__Why: To discover what we can learn from Jeremiah 7:1–28
__With: Journal page 4

> Using the information provided in the leaders' introduction, provide the context for the passage we are about to read from Jeremiah 7.
> Divide the young people into small groups and give everyone a pen and a copy of the journal page. Ask each group to slowly read through Jeremiah 7:1–28. Get them to summarise the main points in the space provided on the journal page.
> Then, again using the space of the journal page, get them to rewrite the following sections as if they were being spoken to the church today.

_ Verses 3–7
_ Verse 19
_ Verses 22–26

> Conclude by discussing either as a whole group or in smaller groups (whatever tends to work best with your young people) the following questions:

___Why do you think the Israelites kept doing the 'rituals' but stopped pleasing God with their lives?
___Do you think we ever do the same? If so, how and why?
___How can we make sure we don't fall into this trap?

__Respond

Idea 1

__Title: Rightly, Wrongly
__Why: To consider how the same action can be done in a way that is both right and wrong
__With: Rightly, Wrongly presentation from www.scriptureunion.org.uk/substance and the means to show it

> Jeremiah 7 has shown us that God required more from the Israelites than just going to the temple (verse 4) – he wanted them to change their lives to do what is right (verse 5). He didn't just want them to offer burnt offerings and sacrifices (verse 22) – he wanted them to obey him in everything (verse 23).
> *Download* the 'Rightly, Wrongly' Presentation and show it to the group. (Either print off the images onto cards or display them on a screen.) For each activity discuss how it could be done 'rightly' (in a way that pleases and honours God) and 'wrongly' (in a way that displeases God).
> Encourage the group to think about the week ahead and list a few things they have to do. Get them to include a variety of activities such as playing football, helping with the Sunday School, attending a youth worship event, going to a friend's birthday party and helping their parents with household chores. In twos or threes ask them to discuss how they can make sure they can do these activities 'rightly'. Encourage them to conclude by praying for each other.

Idea 2

__Title: Number One
__Why: To help the young people consider what is most important in their life
__With: Downloaded video presentation and the means to show it

> Throughout the Old Testament, a common mistake the Israelites make is to worship other gods. In Jeremiah 7, God challenges them through Jeremiah's message and will hopefully challenge the young people too to put God first. After all, we all worship something; the question is what do we worship?
> *Download* the video presentation from www.scriptureunion.org.uk/substance. Show it to the group and encourage them to consider the key questions the video raises:
___What do you worship?
___What is the most important thing in your life?
___Is God first in your life?

> Encourage the young people to prayerfully consider what their top priorities in life are currently. Are they what they should be? If not, what do they think they should be? You might like the group to discuss with one another how they can help each other ensure their priorities are as they should be.
> Finish the session by listening to an appropriate song. For example, Jesus, be the centre (Michael Frye).

Idea 3

__Title: That exiled feeling
__Why: To consider God's presence in difficult times
__With: Reflective music, the means to play it and the meditation from www.scriptureunion.org.uk/substance

> Put some quiet, reflective music on and encourage the young people to reflect on how ...
_ ...the Israelites must have felt in exile.
_ ...Jonah must have felt inside the fish.
_ ...Peter must have felt after he disowned Jesus.
_ ...the disciples must have felt after Jesus was crucified before he rose again.
_ ...you felt last time you knew you had disobeyed God.
_ ...you felt last time you felt far away from God

> *Download* the [poem] [meditation] from www.scriptureunion.org.uk/substance and read it.
> Then encourage the group to pray together. Be particularly sensitive to those who are going through a difficult period at the moment. Provide the young people with the opportunity to chat with a leader after the session.

Journal

There's a recurring theme throughout the Old Testament – it could be summed up by the phrase 'forwards and backwards'. The Israelites would obey God, things would go well for them and they would move forwards. Then they would begin to forget about God, they'd stop obeying him, sometimes they would even begin worshipping other gods, things wouldn't go well for them and they would go backwards. But God would remain faithful, and eventually they would turn back to God (usually after God had delivered them from an enemy), they'd follow him again and once again they'd move forwards. But then, guess what? They'd begin to ignore God again and they would start going backwards once more. It's a cycle that repeats itself throughout the Old Testament.

Does this cycle resonate with you? You attend a festival and you come back on fire for God, but before long you get distracted and you begin to drift. Then you go to a worship event and once again you come back on fire, but it's not long before you begin to slip again.

From the time the Israelites left Egypt until they reached the Promised Land, this 'forwards and backwards' cycle is all too evident. However, in the last session we looked at Moses' motivational speech that explained how they were to be a holy nation, set aside for God. Perhaps now they would get it right? But they didn't. The cycle continued. When the Israelites were going backwards God would provide a 'judge' to get them moving forwards again, but before long they would once again be going backwards. Then the Israelites wanted to be like the other nations and have their own king (before that they were happy for God to be their ruler). They had good kings that would take them forwards, and bad kings that would take them backwards. Eventually civil war broke out and the Israelites were divided into a northern nation (Israel) and southern nation (Judah). The 'forwards and backwards' cycle continued. When they were going backwards God would send prophets to urge them to turn back to God and go forwards. However, as time went on, the prophets were increasingly ignored. Eventually both the northern and southern nations were destroyed and the few remaining Israelites were taken off into exile. It all looked rather bleak. But a remnant remained faithful to God and God continued to work through them. Within a few generations those in exile got to go home and they began rebuilding Jerusalem. They looked forwards to the day that the promised Messiah would come.

Read Jeremiah 7:1–28 slowly and summarise the main points in the space below.

Now imagine that Jeremiah was speaking to the church today.
Have a go at rewriting the following verses for a modern day audience.

Verse 3–7

Verse 19

Verse 22–26

Why do you think the Israelites kept doing the 'rituals' but stopped pleasing God with their lives?

Do you think we ever do the same? If so, how and why?

How can we make sure we don't fall into this trap?

Questions, thoughts and doodles

Incarnation

Aim__To explore why Jesus came to earth.

__Leaders' Introduction

God coming to live amongst us, as the person Jesus Christ, is the pivotal event in human history. It's such a significant event we measure time by it. Never has a person made such an impact on the world, never has a person caused so much controversy and never has so much been at stake on the claims someone has made.

The previous sessions have set the scene for this session; they have introduced why God's mission to earth was necessary. In this session we'll explore the reason for the mission. Jesus came to earth to reveal God to us, teach us how to live and reconcile us to God.

Jesus came to reveal God to us. (Colossians 1:15,19)

God, the creator and ruler of the universe, made himself accessible to us – he made it possible for us to relate to him. He couldn't make himself any bigger, or more powerful to impress us, so instead he made himself smaller – he became one of us, to attract us to him. God didn't primarily reveal himself to the world by shouting at us from heaven – no – he came down to earth and lived as one of us (John 1:18). He didn't deal with the world's sin by sitting up in heaven yelling at us and condemning us for being bad. No, he came down from heaven and dealt with the problem of sin himself. It can be very hard to get our heads around God as a concept, but Jesus, appearing as a human, reveals a God we can begin to get our heads around and can relate to.

Jesus came to teach us how to live. (Matthew 5–7)

Through his actions and words Jesus taught people how to live. He taught people how to live God's way, as God's people in God's world. It was a way of life that seemed to resonate with people, a way of life people were attracted to – not a way of life that was easy, but one which, in so many ways, seemed to make sense. People are still finding the same thing today.

Jesus came to reconcile us with God. (Colossians 1:19–23)

The most significant event in Jesus' life, in fact the most significant event in all human history, was Jesus' death on the cross and his resurrection. In doing this he made it possible for humankind to be reconciled with God. He defeated sin, removing the barrier between us and God and made it possible for all to leave their old lives behind and live new lives in Christ.

In the previous sessions we've considered the Law that God gave his people. In Romans Paul speaks a great deal about the Law and how, because of the Law, we are very conscious of our sin (Romans 3:20). We're never going to be able to be made right with God through keeping the Law – because we're never going to be able to keep it all. Therefore Jesus, through his perfect life, his death and his resurrection, makes it possible for us to be right with God (Romans 3:24–26). This doesn't mean we can throw the Law out because our response to God should be a desire to live lives that please him – the life explained to us in the Law (Romans 6:1–14).

__Begin

Idea 1

__Title: It's Christmas!
__Why: To celebrate God coming to earth
__With: Christmas decorations, music, food and party games

> In this session we'll be exploring God's mission to earth – something we celebrate every year at Christmas. Therefore why not begin the session with a mini Christmas party?
> Decorate the room with Christmas decorations, play Christmas music, eat Christmassy foods and play a few short party games. Then try and settle the group down before introducing the rest of the session!
> This idea will work best if the session is taking place a long time away from Christmas.

Idea 2

__Title: Mission Control!
__Why: To link this session to the previous four
__With: Maybe some props

> In small groups get the young people to prepare short drama sketches.
> The brief is this: imagine you are angels in heaven. As angels you are extremely frustrated about the mess human beings keep getting themselves into (think back over the past four sessions) and are continually shocked that God doesn't just give up on them. And now you've heard a rumour! The word on the heavenly streets is that God is about to do something big;

he apparently has a plan and intends to do something about the problem once and for all. Prepare a short drama that explores what the angels might be talking about.

Idea 3

__Title: Reaction
__Why: To consider how shocking the symbol of the cross is
__With: Images downloaded from www.scriptureunion.org.uk/substance

> *Download* the 'Reaction' images from **www.scriptureunion.org.uk/substance**. Begin by showing them the pictures of Jesus. Get them to discuss what they like/dislike about each image. Ask them to choose which image best represents the 'picture of Jesus' they have in their heads. Encourage them to explain to the group why they chose the image they chose.
> Now show the group the second set of images. Get the young people to shout out the first word that comes into their heads when they see the images. Then let them discuss the image for a little while. Encourage them to explain what feelings each image evokes. Conclude by showing them a selection of images of the cross. After they have discussed these images for a few minutes read 1 Corinthians 1:18. Ask the group what they think this verse means.
> Questions you may like to discuss during this activity include:

__What might attract people to Jesus?
__What might repel people from Jesus?
__In what ways might the cross attract people to Christianity?
__In what ways might the cross repel people from Christianity?
__Why do you think the cross is the most well known Christian symbol?

Idea 4

__Title: Superman vs Jesus
__Why: To begin to think of Jesus as the world's Saviour
__With: *Superman Returns* trailer and the means to show it

> Watch the trailer for *Superman Returns* (there's a link to it on **www.scriptureunion.org.uk/substance**). Then get the group to discuss the similarities and differences between Jesus and Superman. Get them to make notes on large sheets of paper.
> This activity will work best if the group have a wider knowledge of Superman, rather than just what they pick up from watching the trailer.
> Make sure you carry the ideas raised in this section through the rest of the session.

__Explore

Idea 1

__Title: Why did Jesus come to earth?
__Why: To consider why Jesus came to earth (in depth)
__With: Journal page 37 and pens

> Get your group to imagine the scene in heaven...
God is looking at the world he lovingly created and has continued to sustain; he is deeply grieving over the mess people have made of it. God chose to reveal himself to the world through the Israelites, but they keep getting lost and keep missing the point. He knows it's time to go on a mission, the mission he's planned before time began. It's time for him, the creator, the king and the ruler of the universe, to go and live amongst the people he created – as one of them.

> Divide the young people into small groups and encourage them to discuss what Jesus' mission to earth achieved. Get them to jot down their thoughts on a sheet of paper. If they need prompting get them to flick through the four gospels and think about what he did while he was on earth. After a while, gather the groups together and give them the opportunity to feed back and ask any questions that may have arisen. Read John 3:16–21 together before moving on.

> Using the journal page and the ideas from the leaders' introduction, explore the three key reasons why Jesus came to earth.

Idea 2

__Title: Why did Jesus come to earth?
__Why: To consider why Jesus came to earth (basic)
__With: Animation file and the means to show it

> *Download* the animation file from www.scriptureunion.org.uk/substance and show it to your group. This animation will hopefully begin to open up John 3:16–21 with your group.

> Read each section of John 3:16 separately:
___God loved the world so much
___That he gave his one and only Son
___So that whoever believes in him may not be lost,
___But have eternal life.

> After each section, pause, and get the young people to do one of the following things:
___Create a 'freeze frame' in small groups.
___Draw a quick sketch.
___Find a picture from a newspaper that represents it.
___Write a verse of a poem or song.

> Conclude this activity by explaining, discussing or encouraging the young people to think about how we need to respond to John 3:16.

Idea 3

__Title: Do we need a saviour?
__Why: To explore why we need Jesus to save us

__With: *Superman Returns* DVD and the means to show it

> If you showed the trailer for *Superman Returns* at the beginning of this session you may like to continue the Superman theme.

> In the film, Lois Lane wrote an award winning article entitled, *'Why the world doesn't need Superman,'* and during her rooftop conversation with Superman she says, *'The world doesn't need a saviour, and neither do I.'* Then Superman goes on to say *'You wrote that the world doesn't need a saviour. But every day I hear people crying for one.'* If possible show this scene to the group (01:07:28 – 01:13:06).

> Explain to the group that many people today don't accept Jesus as their Saviour, not because they don't believe in him, but because they don't think they need a saviour. They think they are OK and don't consider themselves to be sinners. Therefore, when they hear someone say, 'You need Jesus to save you from your sins,' they think, 'Well, I'm not a sinner – I haven't murdered or raped anyone, or done anything that bad – so I don't need Jesus to save me. I'm an OK person, and I'm sure God will let me into heaven.' As we considered in session two, before we can effectively communicate the good news of Jesus, we have to communicate the bad news of sin – otherwise people will never begin to grasp how important Jesus' death on the cross is.

> Divide the young people into small groups (you may also like to give them paper and pen so they can make notes) and guide them through the following questions before exploring some of the following Bible passages.
___What is the evidence to suggest that the world needs a saviour?
___What is the evidence to suggest that individuals need a saviour?
___If someone asked you to explain why YOU need Jesus to save you, what would you say?
___Why do you think so many people don't accept Jesus as their Saviour? What might you say to them?
___What can we learn from Isaiah 53:6 and Romans 3:23
___How does Romans 3:20 make you feel?
___What is your reaction to John 3:16?

__Respond

Idea 1

__Title: Christ-like attitude
__Why: To reflect on how our attitude is meant to be like Christ's
__With: Music and, if possible, some beanbags and cushions

> We can learn so much about God from the fact that he was willing come down from heaven and live amongst us on earth. Philippians 2:1–11 speaks of how our attitude should be the same as Jesus'.
> Encourage everyone to get comfortable. If there's room get them to lie on the floor. Beanbags or big cushions would be ideal if you have access to any. Put some quiet reflective music on and then read Philippians 2:1–11.
> While you read suggest they reflect on the following questions:
___What do we know about Christ's attitude?
___In what way should our attitude be like Christ's?
___How would you like your attitude to change?

> While the music is still playing conclude by encouraging everyone to say a short prayer thanking Jesus for who he is and what he has done and praying that their attitude would be like his.

Idea 2

__Title: All gone!
__Why: To consider what it means to experience the forgiveness that Christ makes possible

__With: Etcher Sketchers or a video camera

> Jesus enables us to put the past behind us, to leave our sin behind and to have a fresh start. Our new life is now a life in relationship with God – life as it was intended. 2 Corinthians 5:17 says, '*If anyone belongs to Christ, there begins a new creation. The old things have gone; everything is made new!*'
> Use (adapting where necessary) this illustration to communicate how amazing God's forgiveness is.
> When I was younger I was often told that when I got to heaven I would be shown a video tape which revealed all the wrong things I had ever thought, said and done. God would be there watching the film with me (along with my parents and grandma!). However, I'm pleased to say, that this illustration is a load of rubbish! If you are a Christian, if you have asked for forgiveness, if you have accepted that Jesus took all our sin onto himself when he died on the cross, *then the tape has been wiped clean*.
> Illustrate this by setting up a 'Big Brother-style diary room'. Get everyone to go into the room (on their own), sit in front of the video camera and say a few things they have done wrong and want forgiveness for. Tell them that no one will ever watch this tape! After everyone has had their turn destroy the tape in front of them. Do this by either recording over it, or rip the tape out of the cassette and cut it into little pieces.
> Alternatively, give everyone in the group a mini Etcher Sketcher.

Ask them to write a few things on it that they want forgiveness for. Then as they ask God for forgiveness, get them to wipe the Etcher Sketcher clean.

Idea 3

__Title: Revealing Jesus
__Why: To consider how we should reveal Jesus to the world

> Jesus revealed God to the world in a tangible way; in a way that everyone could understand. As Christians we are meant to reveal Jesus to the world. Discuss how you can reveal Jesus to people, through the everyday occurrences of life, over the next week. Make a note of the ideas suggested on a flipchart or a large sheet of paper.
Then, talk about how you might be able to help each other do this. Conclude by praying for one another.

Journal
Journal
Journal
___Journal

God coming to live amongst us, as the person Jesus Christ, is the pivotal event in human history. It's such a significant event we measure time by it. Never has a person made such an impact on the world, never has a person caused so much controversy and never has so much been at stake on the claims someone has made.

The previous sessions have set the scene for this session; they have introduced why God's mission to earth was necessary. In this session we'll explore the reason for the mission.

Jesus came to reveal God to us
(Colossians 1:15, 19)
God, the creator and ruler of the universe, made himself accessible to us – he made it possible for us to relate to him. He couldn't make himself any bigger, or more powerful to impress us, so instead he made himself smaller – he became one of us, to attract us to him. God didn't primarily reveal himself to the world by shouting at us from heaven – no – he came down to earth and lived as one of us (John 1:18). He didn't deal with the world's sin by sitting up in heaven yelling at us and condemning us for being bad. No, he came down from heaven and dealt with the problem of sin himself. It can be very hard to get our heads around God as a concept, but Jesus, appearing as a human, reveals a God we can begin to get our heads around and can relate to.

Jesus came to teach us how to live
(Matthew 5–7)
Through his actions and words Jesus taught people how to live. He taught people how to live God's way, as God's people in God's world. It was a way of life that seemed to resonate with people, a way of life people were attracted to – not a way of life that was easy, but one which, in so many ways, seemed to make sense. People are still finding the same thing today.

Jesus came to reconcile us with God
(Colossians 1:19–23)
The most significant event in Jesus' life, in fact the most significant event in all human history, was Jesus' death on the cross and his resurrection. In doing this he made it possible for humankind to be reconciled with God. He defeated sin, removing the barrier between us and God and made it possible for all to leave their old lives behind and live lives in Christ.

What do you think Jesus' mission to earth achieved?

Jesus came to reveal God to us

(Colossians 1:15,19)

What can we learn about God from looking at the person of Jesus? Why did Jesus make it easier for people to understand what God is like? As Christians we are meant to reveal God to people. What can we learn from the way God reveals himself to us, in terms of how we should reveal God to others?

Jesus came to teach us how to live

(Matthew 5–7: don't feel you have to read it all, just flick through it!)

Flick through the Gospels and make a list of what you consider to be Jesus' 'top ten teaching points'. Why do you think so many people were attracted to Jesus' teaching? What do people think of Jesus' teaching today? Why?

1)
2)
3)
4)
5)
6)
7)
8)
9)
10)

Jesus came to reconcile us with God

(Colossians 1:15,19)

Why do humans need to be reconciled with God?
Why was Jesus able to reconcile us with God?
What's a man dying on a cross 2000 years ago got to do with us today?

Questions, thoughts and doodles

Resurrection

Aim__To consider God's amazing plans for the future.

__Leaders' Introduction

This is the last session in our current series in which we've been looking at some monumental scenes from the Bible. It should come as no surprise to you that this session looks at the final scene – how God's story is going to end. Well, it sort of ends, because the end is actually a new beginning!

As we consider the end and what happens next we enter potentially dangerous territory. There is so much that is unknown about the future, and although the Bible provides us with many glimpses of what's going to happen, it's an area that Christians frequently disagree over. In creating this session, we've tried to stick with the key ideas rather than delve deeply into any particular theological fine print!

Be careful when planning this session. It might be tempting to cover a lot of ground in a very short space of time. It's probably best not to. Using the ideas provided decide exactly what you want the key learning point for this session to be and design the session to suit your group. Although I'm sure many questions will be raised throughout your time together, try to promote clarity and not confusion. But remember, it is OK for questions to be left unanswered.

Here are a few notes on key events that the Bible speaks of in the final scene of God's story.

Christ's Return (Matthew 24:36–51, 1 Corinthians 15:12–28)
Christ is coming back to wrap up this phase of human history. We don't know exactly when and we don't know exactly how. However, the Bible does make it clear that we need to be prepared for this day. According to the Bible, a book that has time and time again proved itself trustworthy, the dead will rise and there will be much more to come after this life.

The Final Judgement (Matthew 25:31–46, 1 Corinthians 3:13–15)
After the dead have been raised there will be judgement. The exact ins-and-outs of this are an area of much discussion and often confusion. However, what is apparent is that everyone will be judged and justice will be done. We believe that our eternal security is in Christ, not what we do and don't do. Therefore, our salvation is secure. However, the Bible certainly implies that we will still have to give an account of how we have lived our lives.

A New Heaven and a New Earth (Revelation 21:1–8)
Jesus makes it possible for us to have eternal life (John 3:16) and this isn't going to be just some spiritual existence that only our souls are part of. We will have new bodies (2 Corinthians 5:1–5) and be part of God's new creation. God will be creating a new heaven and a new earth: a perfect place for us to spend eternity.

A Place of Punishment (Matthew 25:41, Matthew 25:30)
The Bible explains that there are two options for eternity (Matthew 7:13–14): a good option and a bad option, a place of reward and a place of punishment. The subject of hell is one of much disagreement amongst Christians. However, we cannot ignore what the Bible says about punishment, otherwise we will fail to realise just how amazing it is that Jesus rescues us from it.

__Begin

Idea 1

__Title: Happy Endings
__Why: To introduce the idea of endings
__With: The 'Famous Film Endings Quiz' and possibly a prize

> *Download* the 'Famous Film Endings Quiz' from **www.scriptureunion.org.uk/ substance**. Run the quiz by describing (or getting people to act out) the famous film endings and see if the group can guess the film titles. Give a prize to the winning team.
> Encourage the group to discuss what they consider to be some of the best and worst film endings of all time.
> Conclude this section by explaining how, over the past few sessions, we've been looking at some key scenes in God's story – in this session we're going to explore how it's all going to end.

Idea 2

__Title: Temporary
__Why: To introduce the idea that this life is temporary, but eternity is permanent
__With: A few packs of playing cards and a prize

> Divide the group into teams and give each team a pack of playing cards. See which team can build the highest card tower in the set time. Reward the winning team with a prize.
> Conclude by explaining that this life is temporary and very fragile, but as Christians we have the hope of eternity – which is going to be permanent. You may like to read Matthew 6:19–21, 2 Corinthians 5:1–5 and/or the following section from C.S. Lewis' final book in The Chronicles of Narnia, *The Last Battle*:
'For us this is the end of all the stories... But for them it was only the beginning of the real story. All their life in this world... had only been the cover, the title page: now at last they were beginning Chapter One of the Great Story, which no one on earth has read, which goes on for ever and in which every chapter is better than the one before.'

Idea 3

__Title: Futurology
__Why: To illustrate that the future is unknown
__With: Internet access if possible

> In small groups get people to think about what the world will be like in 10 and 100 years time. You may need to direct their discussion and give them some prompts, for example, how will we get around? What will homes be like? What sort of gadgets will be available? What will be the main problems facing the world? If Internet access is a possibility, then perhaps they could look online for some ideas.
> The future is unknown, and humans have proved time and time again that we're not very good at predicting the future, as these quotes indicate:
__*'No one will need more than 637kb of memory for a personal computer.'* [Bill Gates]
__*'We don't like their sound. Groups of guitars are on the way out.'* [Decca record executive on the Beatles]
__*'Everything that can be invented has been invented.'* [Charles Duell, U.S. Office of Patents – 1899]
__*'There is no reason anyone would want a computer in their home.'* [Ken Olson, Digital Equipment Corporation – 1977]
__*'Airplanes are interesting toys but of no military value.'* [Marshall Ferdinand Foch, French Military Strategist and future WW1 commander in 1911]
__*'For the majority of people, the use of tobacco has a beneficial effect.'* [Dr Ian G. MacDonald, LA Surgeon, quoted in Newsweek, November 1969]
__*'Television won't be able to hold on to any market it captures after the first six months. People will soon get tired of staring at a plywood box every night.'* [Darryl F. Zanuck, Head of 20th Century Fox in 1946]

__Explore

Idea 1

__Title: What next?
__Why: To discuss the possibility of life after death
__With: Books, voting slips and if possible Internet access

> This idea is slightly different from the other two Bible engagement ideas and breaks away from the normal *SUbstance* format. This is because it's probably fairly pointless exploring what the Bible has to say about the resurrection of the dead or heaven if your group do not believe that there is life after death.

> Divide the group into two. Get one group to put together a case for there being no life after death and the other to prepare a case for there being life after death. You may like to provide them with a selection of books and/or Internet access to help them. Ideally, have a leader working with each group to help them prepare their arguments.

> Once both groups have prepared their arguments get them to present their case to the other group. Give each group the opportunity to ask the other group questions and then facilitate an orderly debate.

> Read some of the following Bible verses and ask the group for their opinions on them:
__ Ecclesiastes 3:11
__ John 14:1–4
__ 2 Corinthians 5:1–5
__ Hebrews 13:14

> Conclude this idea by giving everyone a voting slip (these can be *downloaded* from www.scriptureunion.org.uk/substance) and ask them to cast their anonymous vote as to whether they believe that there is life after death. Collect the slips, count the vote, and announce the result.

Idea 2

__Title: Travel Agents
__Why: To discover what the Bible has to say about the new heaven and the new earth
__With: Holiday brochures

> Begin by summarising the series by explaining that we've learnt how God created everything and it was amazing. But humans messed it up. We've then seen how God didn't give up on people; he built a nation to reveal himself to the world. But they continually disobeyed him. But still he didn't give up. In fact, he came down to earth to solve the problem once and for all. And the Bible tells us how the epic story of human history is going to end – with a new creation – a new heaven and a new earth – everything restored to how it's meant to be – perfect.

> The Bible gives us several glimpses as to what this new creation, this new heaven and earth is going to be like. This activity aims to help your group explore these.

> Get hold of a selection of holiday brochure from travel agents. Give the group a few minutes to browse through them and decide where they would most like to go for their next holiday.

> Divide the group into twos and threes and get them to create a short paragraph, like you'd find in a holiday brochure, describing what the new heaven and new earth is going to be like. The following Bible passages will be a good starting point:
_ John 14:2–4
_ 2 Corinthians 5:1–5
_ Revelation 19:6–10
_ Revelation 21:1–7

> The Bible explains that when it comes to the end of the story and eternity, there are two options – a good option (heaven) and a bad option (hell). In recent years there has been a fair amount of disagreement amongst Christians as to the exact nature of hell. However, you may like to repeat the above exercise, but this time create a short paragraph based on what the Bible says about hell.
_ Matthew 25:30
_ Matthew 25:41
_ Mark 9:48
_ Revelation 14:11

> Conclude this idea by getting the young people to discuss, write on a big sheet of paper or paint pictures of what they are most looking forward to about the new heaven and the new earth.

Idea 3

__Title: The end
__Why: To explore what the Bible has to say about the end of the world as we know it
__With: Journal Page 43, and other background materials (if possible)

> Divide the young people into four groups. Explain to them that over the next few minutes each group will be exploring what the Bible has to say about one component of the end of the world as we know it.
__ Christ's Return
__ The Final Judgement
__ A New Heaven and New Earth
__ A Place of Punishment

> Using the questions, Bible passage and other pointers provided on the journal page, get each group to prepare a short presentation on their component. If possible provide additional background materials.

> As each group presents what they have found out to the wider group, encourage people to make notes on the journal page. The presentations are bound to raise questions – explore these with the group before moving on.

__Respond

Idea 1

__Title: Space
__Why: To provide space for reflection, prayer and chat about the issues raised during this session
__With: Refreshments, music, path making materials (!) and maybe paint

> We've looked at some big issues in this session! Thinking about the end times can be both encouraging and scary at the same time! Why not end the session with some space, with a variety of options for the young people to dip in and out of? Here are some ideas:

> Have some chilled music playing in the background and a selection of tasty snacks and refreshing drinks. Write out the verses found in Revelation 19:7–10 and display them next to the food and drink.

> Attach a big sheet of paper on the wall and encourage young people to write down any questions this session has raised for them. Although it's likely there are no easy answers to many of these questions, perhaps you could explore some of them in a future session?

> Write out Revelation 21:4–5 on a large sheet of paper, and encourage people to draw or paint pictures around the words to illustrate what these verses mean to them.

> Set aside a corner where young people can just sit and think. Have another corner where young people can chat and/or pray with a leader.

> Create a narrow path on the floor (out of string, paper or whatever you think will work best). Ask the young people to write down the names of friends that are not Christians on slips of paper, and lay them on the path. Encourage people to spend time walking along the path praying for the names. At the end of the session collect up the slips of paper and divide them amongst the young people. Ask the young people to pray regularly for these people.

Idea 2

__Title: Present Heaven
__Why: To explore what it means to live as 'citizens of heaven' now
__With: Possibly a passport to use as an illustration

> Explain to the group that when people speak about 'heaven' today they are usually referring to the place where we will go when we die – something that will happen in the future. (This is not wrong, and it's what we have being doing during this session!) However, when the Jews, who made up most of Jesus' original audience, spoke of heaven, they were usually referring to the present place where God was – his throne room from where he rules the world. Heaven is not just a future hope, it's a present reality.

> Get your group to read the following Bible verses and discuss what they think they mean. Alternatively you could prepare a short talk.
__Philippians 3:20
__Matthew 6:10

> Ask the group to discuss in pairs what it practically means to 'live as citizens of heaven' (living with Jesus as king of their lives) and how they think they can 'bring heaven to earth' (as God's will is done on earth as it is in heaven).

> Conclude by writing their specific ideas on a large piece of paper and praying for one another.

Idea 3

__Title: The choice
__Why: To communicate to young people that a choice has to be made
__With: 'Wide vs Narrow' animation file and the means to show it.

> Life offers us many choices; eternity offers us just two. Why not conclude this session by clearly and concisely explaining the gospel message to your group and communicating the consequences of accepting or rejecting Jesus? Use Matthew 7:13–14 as the basis of this. You may also like to **Download** the 'Wide vs Narrow' animation file from **www.scriptureunion. uk/substance** and show it to your group.

> You need to choose what you think will be the best way to communicate the gospel message to your group. However, you may want to use one of the well known illustrations recommended on **www.scriptureunion.org.uk/ substance.**

Idea 4

__Title: Temporary living
__Why: To think practically about what 'temporary living' involves
__With: Sticky labels

> This life is temporary; what's to come will last forever. As Christians we need to live our lives in the light of eternity.
> Read and discuss Matthew 6:19–21, 2 Corinthians 5:1–5 and Philippians 3:20–21.
> Then give everyone in the group about 20 sticky labels and a pen. Get them to write the word 'temporary' on all the sticky labels. Encourage them, when they get home, to stick these labels on various things they own, to remind them that they are only temporary. For example: computer, music collection, MP3 player, mobile phone, and jewellery.

Journal
__Journal
Journal

This is the last session in our current series in which we've been looking at some monumental scenes from the Bible. It should come as no surprise to you that this session looks at the final scene – how God's story is going to end. Well, it sort of ends, because the end is actually a new beginning!

Christ's return

Christ is coming back to wrap up this phase of human history. We don't know exactly when and we don't know exactly how. However, the Bible does make it clear that we need to be prepared for this day. According to the Bible, a book that has time and time again proved itself trustworthy, the dead will rise and there will be much more to come after this life.

The final judgement

After the dead have been raised there will be judgement. The exact ins-and-outs of this are an area of much discussion and often confusion. However, what's apparent is that everyone will be judged and justice will be done. We believe that our eternal security is in Christ, not what we do and don't do. Therefore, our salvation is secure. However, the Bible certainly implies that we will still have to give an account of how we have lived our lives.

A new heaven and earth

Jesus makes it possible for us to have eternal life (John 3:16) and this isn't going to be just some spiritual existence that only our souls are part of. We will have new bodies (2 Corinthians 5:1–5) and be part of God's new creation. God will be creating a new heaven and a new earth: a perfect place for us to spend eternity.

A place of punishment

The Bible explains that there are two options for eternity (Matthew 7:13–14): a good option and a bad option, a place of reward and a place of punishment. The subject of hell is one of much disagreement amongst Christians. However, we cannot ignore what the Bible says about punishment, otherwise we will fail to realise just how amazing it is that Jesus rescues us from it.

Christ's return

Matthew 24:36–51
1 Corinthians 15:12–28

How does knowing that Christ will one day return make you feel? How should knowing about this effect how we live our lives? What do you find scary or bizarre about this talk of 'the resurrection of the dead'? What do you find exciting about it?

The final judgement

Matthew 25:14–46
1 Corinthians 3:13–15

What would you say to someone who is worried about the final judgement? How should knowing about the final judgement affect how we live our lives?

A new heaven and a new earth

Revelation 21:1–8
2 Corinthians 5:1–5

Can you find out the significance of there being 'no sea' as part of the new heaven and earth? What excites you most about this picture? How should knowing about the new heaven and earth affect how we live our lives?

A place of punishment

Matthew 7:13–14
Matthew 25:30,41

How does the Bible's teaching on hell make you feel? What questions does it raise for you? Does it alter how you see Jesus' death on the cross? How should knowing about this place of punishment affect how we live our lives?

Questions, thoughts and doodles

Spirituality

God wants us to live our lives in relationship with him and he wants us to make a difference with our lives. In this module we'll be discovering four aspects of the Christian life that will enable us to get closer to God and equip us to make a difference.

Bible

Aim__To explore why the Bible is important and how we should use it in our lives.

__Leaders' Introduction

The Bible, the world's all-time best-seller, is a truly remarkable book. But is it one we all too often take for granted? Throughout the world many people travel many miles, on foot, each week to hear it read. Many people would make huge sacrifices to own a copy of the book in their own language. For us, well, we often have several copies, but how frequently does this book, the book that we believe contains God's words, remain unread?

This session will give you an opportunity to encourage your group to consider their Bible reading habits. But before you do that, this might be a good opportunity for you to think about how effective your own Bible reading is.

The primary passage we will be exploring in this session is 2 Timothy 3:14–17. It is part of a letter the apostle Paul, a seasoned expert in doctrine, church planting and developing leaders, wrote to Timothy, a young pastor in the early church. The letter is written about 30 years after Jesus' resurrection and the church is rapidly growing and is trying to find its feet in a climate of persecution, scepticism and distrust. In verse 10 Paul speaks about his way of life, a way of life that Timothy has adopted. Their goals are faith, patience and love, but Paul, currently writing from prison, knows only too well, that this way of life leads to a great deal of persecution.

Therefore Paul urges his young prodigy, Timothy, to keep following the teachings he has learned, no matter what (verse 14). He then goes on to succinctly explain why the Scriptures are so important.

He explains how Scripture leads to wisdom that in turns leads to salvation (verse 15). It's Scripture that reveals God's love for us. It shows the problem of our disobedience and lays out God's plan for salvation – how our sins can be forgiven and our relationship with God restored.

Paul then goes on to explain how important the Scriptures, which are inspired by God, are for teaching, showing us what is wrong, correcting faults and teaching us how to live right (verse 16).

There are several other passages that we can find in the Bible that echo the same truths. Why not read Psalm 119 before leading this session? It's a Psalm that speaks about the importance of listening to and obeying God's Word.

Reading the Bible is a huge privilege and it can help us so much as we seek to follow Jesus. However, as we read the Bible we must remember we don't do so just to gain head knowledge; we do so to discover who Jesus is, so we can deepen our relationship with him and live our lives in a way that pleases him. As Paul says in the beginning of his letter to Titus, it's about *'knowledge of the truth that leads to godliness'* (Titus 1:1 NIV). Knowledge and reading the Bible isn't the end – it's the means to an end – a relationship with Jesus and living a life that pleases him.

Effective Bible reading isn't just about reading the Bible and learning the stories. Effective Bible reading is about applying it to our lives; it's about becoming more like Jesus. This session isn't primarily about getting the young people in your group to read more Bible verses each day, it's about helping them understand why the Bible is so important (which will hopefully provide some motivation) and how they can best apply the Bible to their lives (which will hopefully make reading the Bible much more meaningful).

Personal Bible reading can be of huge benefit to our spirituality and it is core to Scripture Union's ministry. Visit **www.scriptureunion.org.uk** to see a range of Bible reading products we produce to help people effectively engage with the Bible.

__Begin

Idea 1

__Title: Out-of-date?
__Why: To explore whether your group think the Bible is out-of-date
__With: Downloaded pictures

> *Download* the pictures for this activity from **www.scriptureunion. org.uk/substance**. Get the young people to group the photographs as to whether they think what they show is out-of-date or up-to-date.
> Next, encourage them to discuss what makes something out-of-date or up-to-date and why some things date quickly, while other things never go out-of-date.
> Conclude by discussing what they think about the Bible.

___Do they consider it to be out-of-date? Why (not)?
___In what ways do they think the Bible is out-of-date?
___In what ways is it most certainly not?
___Why do many people perceive the Bible as being an out-of-date and irrelevant book? What can we do about this?

Idea 2

__Title: Perceptions
__Why: To consider how we view the Bible
__With: Downloaded animation file and the means to show it

> *Download* and show the group the animation file. It aims to explore how people perceive the Bible. For example, is it a rulebook, a loaf of bread, a love letter, a fantasy story or a party invitation?

> At the end, pause the animation (so all the images remain on the screen) and encourage the young people to discuss, in twos and threes, what image(s) best represent what they think of the Bible. Why is this? How does this affect how you approach the Bible? Also get them to talk about what their friends think about the Bible.

Idea 3

__Title: Influence
__Why: To consider how much influence reading the Bible has in our lives
__With: Calculators, protractors, maybe even a computer!

> Ask everyone in the group to write on some paper how much time they spend doing various activities in a normal week. Much of the time will be taken up with sleeping, and school, college or work, but get them to think about what else they do and to include activities such as reading, listening to music, shopping, watching TV and playing sport.
> Once they have a list of all the activities, get them to work out the percentage of time in their lives they spend doing these things. (Divide the time spent in hours by the total number of hours in a week (168) and then multiply by 100.) If you have protractors, or access to a computer with spreadsheet software you could create a Venn diagram for each person – make sure you do one yourself too! (*Download* a sample of this activity from

www.scriptureunion.org.uk/ substance.)
> Ask the group to discuss with each other what their lists/Venn diagrams reveal. What does it say about their priorities? Do they think they are spending their time wisely? What activities are having the greatest impact and influence on their lives? Which activities is God involved in? How much time are they spending reading the Bible each week? How much is this influencing them?
> You may like to *download* the 'Bible Verse and Advertising Slogan' quiz from **www. scriptureunion.org.uk/ substance**. This is likely to reveal that we know a lot more about advertising slogans than we do Bible verses. Discuss with your group whether they think this is a problem.

__Explore

Idea 1

__Title: Marketing Campaign
__Why: To consider why the Bible is so important
__With: That depends on how creative you want to be

> Divide the group into threes or fours and explain that they are marketing executives. Their job is to put together an advertising campaign for the Bible. They have to prepare a presentation to 'sell' the Bible to people who are very sceptical about it. They must come up with some possible marketing straplines, ideas for a poster campaign and a TV advert. (Depending on your time constraints you might want them to produce posters and film their TV advert. Make sure any filming adheres to your churches' Child Protection Policy.)
> Give them the following Bible passages to look up before they start. 2 Timothy 3:14–17, Luke 1:3–4, John 20:30,31, Romans 15:4 and Psalm 119:9,15,18.
> After the young people have presented their marketing campaigns (as creatively as your time and resources allow) to the wider group, discuss why the Bible is so vital and important to our lives. Alternatively you may like to prepare a short talk.

Idea 2

__Title: Where would you go?
__Why: To communicate that the Bible is a good place to go for guidance
__With: Resource page 76

> On a large piece of paper ask your group to list as many different places where people look for guidance. (For example, horoscopes, parents and friends.) After a while, broaden the question to include all the things that influence the decisions we make. Then get the group to discuss which of these they think are positive and which they think are negative. Then ask them to circle the ones that are the most significant influences in their lives.
> In pairs, read 2 Timothy 3:14–17 and discuss why the Bible is a good place to go for guidance. Ask each pair to share their thoughts with the rest of the group.
> Encourage anyone who wants to tell the group of a time where the Bible has guided them. You might like to give a few young people and leaders advance warning of this so they could prepare something before the session.
> Give everyone in the group a copy of resource page 76. In pairs get them to respond to the various 'problems' using the Bible as the basis of the guidance given.
> Conclude this section by encouraging the group to say a few short prayers thanking God for guiding us.

Idea 3

__Title: Teach it
__Why: To consider why reading the Bible is so important
__With: That depends on how creative you want to be

> It's often said that the best way to really learn something is to teach it to others. Why not get your group to prepare a ten minute presentation to teach 7-11 or 11-14-year-olds why it is so important to read the Bible?
> Ask them to use 2 Timothy 3:14–17 and a few verses from Psalm 119 (there's 176 to choose from!) as the basis for their presentation. They could include drama, talks, testimony, illustrations, games and PowerPoint presentations. It really depends on the time and resources you have available.
> Ideally arrange it so that your group can actually present what they prepare to the appropriate age group.

__Respond

Idea 1

__Title: Essential Skills
__Why: To teach young people three essential Bible reading skills
__With: Journal page and maybe a few Mr Men books

> Ask the group to discuss why they think the Bible can often be very difficult to understand. Then use the journal page and the following ideas to talk about three essential Bible reading skills.

> **Know what you're reading.** Explain to the group that you would read a love letter very differently from how you would read a text book and you'd read a novel very differently from how you would read an instruction manual. The Bible contains a wide variety of styles of writing. It's important that you understand what type of writing you are reading, as this will affect your understanding of the passage and how you apply it to your lives.

> Get your group to look up the Bible passages found on the journal page and decide what type of writing they are. The answers can be found on page 80!

> **Know where it fits.** Imagine that you were reading a Harry Potter book. You read a few pages from the middle, then a couple of paragraphs from near the beginning and then you read a chapter towards the end. It probably wouldn't make much sense, would it? Many people say the Bible doesn't make much sense, and that's hardly surprising because this

is how many people read the Bible! However, with the Bible it's not that simple, because it's not all laid out in chronological order. However, it's important that you know where the bit you are reading fits into the big picture – the overarching story of the Bible. Get your group to see if they can put the key scenes of the Bible mentioned on the journal page in order.

> To illustrate the importance of order, purchase a few Mr Men books. Cut off the spines and shuffle the pages. Then get your group to put them back in the correct order!

> **Know what to do about it.** Explain to your group that when they read a Bible passage they should always be thinking about what they should learn from it. Encourage them to consider the context, principle and application.

___ **Context:** What the author wanted to communicate to the original audience. Is it specific instructions for them in their context, or does it apply to us today?

___ **Principle:** What is the key principle, the key learning point, in the passage?

___ **Application:** How can we put into practice what we have just read, in our own lives?

> Divide the young people into twos and threes and give each group one of the Bible passages.

Idea 2

__Title: Making it work
__Why: To encourage one another to set aside time for

effective Bible reading
__With: Maybe some sample Bible reading notes

> Most people don't plan not to read the Bible; it's just that it can be so hard to get into a routine that works. Conclude the session by discussing this and related issues. Encourage the young people to share what they have found works for them and hopefully the group will learn from one another. Some of the questions below could help to structure the discussion. Finish by coming up with a plan of action.

___ Do you find it easy or difficult to spend time reading the Bible regularly? Why?

___ When do you read the Bible?

___ How do you approach your time with the Bible? Do you use any form of study notes? Which ones? Do you find they help? Why (not)?

___ What do you think would make your Bible reading more effective?

___ As a group how can we help each other read the Bible more effectively?

> You may like to have a range of Bible reading notes for the young people to look at. Perhaps you could get the group to evaluate them using a criteria (a number of questions) created by the group.

Idea 3

__Title: Divinely breathed
__Why: To reflect on the Bible as God's Word
__With: Possibly some ambient music and the means to play it

> Explain that 2 Timothy 3:16 uses an interesting phrase. The NCV translates it as 'given by God'; it literally means 'God-breathed'. But what does this mean? It is probably easier to say what it doesn't mean. It doesn't mean that the writers of the Bible were put into a trance and used as some form of human typewriter! Rather, they were moved by God and inspired by the Holy Spirit to write what we have today.

> To remind ourselves of this use the following meditation that uses breathing as the focus. Explain to the group that this meditation follows a simple two sentence rhythm. On the first sentence the group should exhale and on the second sentence they should inhale. As they do both, encourage them to focus on the words that are being read. You may like to have some ambient music playing while you do this meditation. Make sure you read the meditation slowly, and you may like to repeat it several times.

__ *[Exhale]* Take the things that influence my life
__ *[Inhale]* Fill me with your Word
__ *[Exhale]* Take the time that counts my life
__ *[Inhale]* Fill me with your Word
__ *[Exhale]* Take the distractions that divert my life
__ *[Inhale]* Fill me with your Word
__ *[Exhale]* Take my weakness that stops my discipline
__ *[Inhale]* Fill me with your Word
__ *[Exhale]* Take my knowledge that is unwise
__ *[Inhale]* Fill me with your Word
__ *[Exhale]* Take my apology that says I'm sorry
__ *[Inhale]* Fill me with your Word
__ Amen.

Journal
__Journal Journal
Journal

Do you sometimes read a passage from the Bible and think, 'What?!!' 'What on earth does that mean?' or 'Surely I can't learn anything from that?' Well, perhaps these three essential Bible reading skills will help you!

Know what you're reading

You would read a love letter very differently from how you would read a text book and you'd read a novel very differently from how you would read an instruction manual. The Bible contains a wide variety of styles of writing. It's important that you understand what type of writing you are reading, as this will affect your understanding of the passage and how you apply it to your lives.

Know where it fits

Imagine that you were reading a Harry Potter book. You read a few pages from the middle and then a couple of paragraphs from near the beginning and then you read a chapter towards the end. It probably wouldn't make much sense, would it? Many people say the Bible doesn't make much sense, and that's hardly surprising because this is how many people read the Bible! However, with the Bible it's not that simple, because it's not all laid out in chronological order. However, it's important that you know where the bit you are reading fits into the big picture, the overarching story of the Bible.

Know what to do about it

Whenever you read a Bible passage you should always be thinking about what you can learn from it and how it should impact your life. One way to approach this is to consider the context, principle and application of every Bible passage you read.

Context: What the author wanted to communicate to the original audience. Is it specific instructions for them in their context, or does it apply to us today?

Principle: What is the key principle, the key learning point, in the passage?

Application: How can we put into practice what we have just read in our own lives?

> Why can it sometimes be difficult to understand the Bible?

Know what you're reading

What type of writings are the following passages?

1) Revelation 1:12–15
2) Deuteronomy 18:9,10
3) Matthew 13:44
4) Proverbs 14:30
5) Joshua 1:1,2
6) Philippians 4:2–4
7) Amos 1:6,7
8) Psalm 98:8,9

a) Parables
b) Letters
c) Apocalyptic
d) Law
e) History
f) Song
g) Wise sayings
h) Prophecy

Know where it fits

Can you put these key 'scenes' of the Bible in order? (Without looking in a Bible, of course!)

1) Gideon defeats the Midianites.
2) Jesus is born.
3) God promises that he'll make Abram's family into a great nation.
4) The Holy Spirit comes on the day of Pentecost.
5) Daniel is thrown into a den of lions.
6) Joseph becomes Pharaoh's number two and diverts a national disaster.
7) Nehemiah builds a wall.
8) Joshua leads the people of Israel into the Promised Land.
9) A snake tempts Eve to eat the wrong piece of fruit.
10) The city of Jerusalem was destroyed by the Babylonians.

Know what to do about it

Read one of the following Bible passages and consider the context, principle and application.
Leviticus 14:33–57, Psalm 23. Daniel 1, Amos 5:21–24, Matthew 20:1–16,
1 Corinthians 11:17–34, Revelation 3:1–6.

 Context

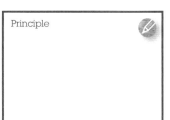 Principle

 Application

Questions, thoughts and doodles

Prayer

Aim__To explore why and how we should pray.

__Leaders' Introduction

Prayer is one of the many great privileges we have as Christians. This session aims to communicate how prayer isn't primarily about getting what we want; it's about developing a relationship with God – a relationship that will change us, and our priorities, as our desires align with God's desires.

How you approach this session will very much depend on how those in your group currently regard prayer. As always there are a variety of ideas that will help you create a session that engages, encourages and challenges those in your group – whatever stage they are at on their Christian journey. This session provides an excellent opportunity for the group to learn from one another as they discuss their experiences of prayer.

This session is likely to raise some difficult questions. For example, 'Why didn't God heal my mum?' For many of these questions there are no easy answers. It's important that we remember that prayer isn't a formula, it's a relationship, and relationships are complicated.

At the heart of this session is the Lord's Prayer. Let's briefly consider, line by line, what we can learn about prayer from it.

Our Father in heaven…
Jesus tells us to call God, 'Father'. The actual word he would have used was 'Abba' which we can best translate as 'Daddy'. Prayer is about building a personal relationship with God. Jesus compared it to a relationship between a child and a loving parent. But it also acknowledges that God is in heaven – he's above us. As we pray we should approach God humbly, acknowledging our weakness and his strength.

May your name always be kept holy…
This is about acknowledging and thanking God for who he is. Yes, God wants us to come to him in the same way as children approach their parents, but we must never forget who God is – the creator and king of the entire universe.

May your kingdom come and what you want be done, here on earth as it is in heaven…
This is about ensuring our priorities are in line with God's. Prayer shouldn't be about getting what we want to happen; it should be about getting what God wants to happen. It's important that we discover what God wants in the Bible and through the prompting of his Holy Spirit – this will help us pray for the things that God wants us to pray for.

Give us the food we need for each day…
God wants us to ask him for things – just like children would ask their parent for things. But notice how Jesus uses food (most versions say bread) as the example – something essential. When we ask God for things, are we asking him for things we need or things we want?

Forgive us for our sins, just as we have forgiven those who sinned against us…
When we pray we should confess our sins to God, asking and receiving his forgiveness. Also notice that prayer isn't just about God doing things; we have to do things as well. God forgives us, so he also expects us to forgive others. Prayer is one way we can take action, but it's not an opportunity for us to be irresponsible towards the problems we see around us. It's good to pray that God would 'help those experiencing injustice'. But how do you think God might answer those prayers? By telling us to do something about those problems!

And do not cause us to be tempted, but save us from the Evil One…
God rules, but the devil is at work trying to influence us. God is infinitely more powerful than the devil; therefore it makes sense to ask for his protection. Prayer prepares us for the battles we face day by day.

__Begin

Idea 1

__Title: Prayer Advertising
__Why: To explore what young
   people think about prayer
__With: That depends on how
   creative you are feeling!

> Option 1: Show a couple of
mobile phone commercials. Then,
in small groups, get the young
people to create their own 'TV
Commercial' to advertise prayer.
Once they have created their
'commercials' ask each group to
present theirs to everyone else.
> Option 2: *Download* a list of
past and present mobile phone
companies' advertising slogans
from **www.scriptureunion.org.uk/
substance**. Divide your group into
teams and have a competition
to see who can match the most
slogans to the correct companies.
Then ask each team to come up
with an 'advertising slogan' for
prayer.

Idea 2

__Title: Prayer Poll
__Why: To find out what people
   think about prayer

> This idea requires advance
planning!
Most surveys reveal that a lot
of people pray. So why not get
your group to do some research
at school or in the high street?
(Make sure all the necessary
precautions are taken and if
you need permission from your
local council make sure you
obtain it.) *Download* some

sample questionnaires from
**www.scriptureunion.org.uk/
substance**.
> Discuss as a group what
information you would like to
collect and what questions you
could ask. Perhaps you could
take a video camera with you
and interview people so the
whole group can watch people's
responses.

Idea 3

__Title: Help!
__Why: To illustrate that some
   people just don't like to ask
   for help
__With: Photocopy of page 77, a
   blindfold, a pen and a prize

> Photocopy the maze found
on page 77 onto a large piece
of paper (ideally A3). Ask for a
volunteer and give them a marker
pen. Tell them that they have to
work their way around the maze.
Promise a prize for the person
who does it in the quickest time
with the neatest line. HOWEVER!
Just before they are about to start
blindfold them.
> Once they have made their
attempt ask for another volunteer.
Keep doing this (as time allows!)
until someone asks for help! If no
one asks for help, suggest the last
volunteer does!
> Conclude by explaining how
many people just don't like to ask
for help. At the heart of prayer
is the idea of us asking for help,
acknowledging that we are weak
and God is strong. If we think we
are 'self-sufficient' and don't need
God's help, we're not likely to
pray. There are many people who

try everything they can first, and
only turn to God as a last resort.
Read Philippians 4:6.

Idea 4

__Title: It's good to talk!
__Why: To introduce the idea
   of prayer as building a
   relationship with God

> Ask everyone to answer this
question: If you could have
lunch with any famous person
(past or present) who would it
be and why? Then explain that
meeting and speaking with
someone famous would give us
the opportunity to find out lots
about them and begin to build an
actual relationship with them.
> Do a survey (be as creative as
you can be) to find out some of
the following information:
__What's the longest phone call
   you've ever had?
__How many text messages do
   you send in an average week?
__On average, how long do you
   spend on MSN (or equivalent)
   each day?

> Discuss these questions:
__Why do we enjoy talking to our
   friends?
__What happens when we don't
   talk to our friends for a while?

> All this should introduce a key
reason why we should pray – to
build a relationship with God.
Conclude by discussing these two
questions:
__Why should we pray?
__What does our lack of prayer
   say about what we think about
   a) ourselves and b) God?

__Explore

Idea 1

__Title: Rewrite
__Why: To get the group thinking about the Lord's Prayer

> In twos or threes get everyone to rewrite the Lord's Prayer in modern language. They may like to do this in text language, as a song or maybe even a rap. When they share their version with the wider group, encourage them to explain why they have used the words they have. This will hopefully get them to really think about the meaning behind the words in the Lord's Prayer.

Idea 2

__Title: How should we pray?
__Why: To consider how we should approach prayer with the right attitude
__With: Animation file and the means to show it

> In small groups discuss the characteristics of a 'bad prayer'. Then discuss the characteristics of a 'good prayer'. Write down the good and bad characteristics on two large pieces of paper.
> *Download* the animation file from **www.scriptureunion.org. uk/substance** and show it to your group. And/or read Matthew 6:5–8 and Luke 18:9–14.
> Discuss (in their small groups) what we can learn from these passages and modify the lists of good and bad characteristics as necessary.
> Conclude by discussing, as a whole group, what implications these passages have for group

prayer. (Although Matthew 6:6 says that we should close the door and pray in secret, verses such as Acts 2:42 reveal that group prayer is appropriate. However, we certainly need to learn from the principles laid out in Matthew 6:5–8.)

Idea 3

__Title: What should we pray?
__Why: To think about what our prayers should include
__With: Journal page 57

> Ask everyone to make a list of the sort of things they've included in their prayers over the past few days. There is space for them to do this on the journal page.
> Put that list aside for a few moments and encourage everyone to answer the following questions (they are deliberately vague).
___What do you want?
___What does God want?
Then, compare the two lists. How similar are they? What are the main differences?
> Again make a note of what everyone says. Then compare the two lists. How similar are they? What are the main differences?
> How we respond to the question, 'What do you want?' can say a lot about our priorities. From the two lists summarise God's 'top three priorities' and our 'top three priorities' – be honest. There'll be an opportunity later to discuss aligning our priorities with God's priorities.
> Explain how the content of our prayers can reveal a great deal about our focus and priorities. Ask the young people to consider

what the content of their prayers reveal about their focus and priorities. Also get them to think about what they can learn from the list about how they view God, themselves and other people. Introduce the next part of this section by saying that the Lord's Prayer provides us with an excellent model for prayer.
> Read Matthew 6:9–13. Then, using the journal page and the information in the leaders' introduction, discuss what we can learn about prayer from the Lord's Prayer.

Idea 4

__Title. Unanswered prayers
__Why: To explore why sometimes prayers appear to go unanswered

> Encourage people to share with the group prayers that they believe God has answered. Then encourage people to share prayers that it appears God hasn't answered.
> Spend some time discussing why God might not always answer our prayers in the way that we want or expect.
> Use the following ideas to prepare a short talk on this difficult and sometimes distressing subject. Pause at various points for questions and discussion.
> Matthew 7:7–8 seems to suggest that whatever we ask for, we will get. However, we all know from experience that this is not the case. We've all asked God for things that we've never received.
> If we've been praying for a new computer for ages and don't

get one, we'll probably cope. But sometimes it can be much harder to accept. Think about the person who has been praying that their mum or dad will be healed. They don't get healed and end up dying. This is really tough. There are no easy answers.
> God might not answer all our prayers in the way we want him to, but he does listen, and respond, to all our prayers. There's basically three ways he can respond: 'Yes', 'No' or 'Later'. Matthew 7:9–11 is an excellent illustration. It compares prayer with a child asking his parents for something. There are two things I would like to draw out from these verses.
Firstly, 'Amen' is not the same as 'Abracadabra!' Prayer isn't a formula. It's not about saying the right words, in the right order so that we get the answer we want. Prayer is about us building a relationship with our heavenly Father.
> Secondly, God will not give us things that will harm us. Jesus explains that if a child asks for a fish, a loving father won't give him a snake. This is good, because a snake could do a lot of harm. But equally the reverse is true. If a child asks his loving father for a snake, the father is unlikely to give it to him because he knows that a snake could hurt his child, whom he loves very much. The same is true when we ask God for things – he won't give us something which will harm us or we are not ready for. Hence, he often responds to our prayer by saying 'No' or 'Later'. As Jean Ingelow once said, *'I have lived to thank God that not all my prayers have been answered.'*

__Respond

Idea 1

__Title: Pray for the world
__Why: An opportunity to pray
for issues facing the world
__With: Newspapers, big sheets
of paper, scissors and glue

> Divide the young people into small groups and give each group a big sheet of paper, a few newspapers, scissors and glue. Get them to cut out headlines, pictures and short articles of things they would like to pray for. If you have several small groups doing this get one group to focus on local news, one national news and another international news.
> Once the collages have been completed, ask the young people to spend some time praying for the issues on their collage. You could do this as creatively as you want to. After a while, rotate the groups so everyone prays for all the issues.

Idea 2

__Title: Pray for each other
__Why: An opportunity to pray
for each other
__With: A4 paper and pens

> Give everyone a sheet of A4 paper and get them to write their names on it along with a prayer request. Then get them to pass the piece of paper to the person sitting next to them. Everyone should now have someone else's piece of paper. Tell them to write their name on this new piece of paper along with the same (or different) prayer request. Keep

repeating this until everyone has written on every piece of paper.
> Encourage the group to take this piece of paper home and pray for each other during the coming weeks.
> It may also be appropriate to exchange phone numbers and/or email addresses so you can exchange prayer and praise requests during the week. You could even set up a prayer chain. Make sure that you do this idea in a way that adheres to your church's Child Protection Policy.

Idea 3

__Title: A prayerful life
__Why: To help each other
develop more effective prayer
lives

> It often appears that most Christians know they should pray, but many find it really hard to actually make time to do it. Discuss, in groups of three or four, these questions:
___Why can setting time aside for prayer be so difficult?
___What are some of the things that distract you when you pray?

> Read Mark 1:35 and Mark 6:46. Explain that these are just two examples of Jesus taking himself off to pray, one at the beginning of what was to be a busy day, and one at the end of a busy day. In their groups ask the young people to discuss some of these questions:
___Why do you think Jesus often withdrew from his disciples and the crowds to pray? What

should we learn from this?
___Why is it a good idea to begin the day with prayer?
___Why is it a good idea to end the day with prayer?
___How could you set aside time at the beginning and end of each day?
___What can you do to help yourself stay focused?

> Encourage your group not just to isolate prayer for one or two 'slots' each day. Instead live the whole of life with a prayerful attitude. Keep acknowledging that you need God's help, keep asking for his guidance and keep thanking him for all the good things you see around you. A famous preacher called Smith Wigglesworth said, 'I never pray for more than fifteen minutes, but I never go more than fifteen minutes without praying.'
> Encourage your group to say 'breath prayers'. Throughout the day say short, one or two sentence, prayers. When you see something good, thank God for it. When you see someone in trouble or hurting, pray for them. When you hear about something on the news, pray for the situation.
> Conclude by discussing, as a whole group, how you can help each other lead prayerful lives.

Journal Journal
__Journal
Journal

The Lord's Prayer can teach us so much about prayer: let's look at it line by line.

Our Father in heaven…
Jesus tells us to call God, 'Father'. The actual word he would have used was 'Abba' which we can best translate as 'Daddy'. Prayer is about building a personal relationship with God. Jesus compared it to a relationship between a child and a loving parent. But it also acknowledges that God is in heaven – he's above us. As we pray we should approach God humbly, acknowledging our weakness and his strength.

May your name always be kept holy…
This is about acknowledging, and thanking, God for who he is. Yes, God wants us to come to him as a child approaches his parents, but we must never forget who God is –the creator and king of the entire universe.

May your kingdom come and what you want be done, here on earth as it is in heaven…
This is about ensuring our priorities are in line with God's. Prayer shouldn't be about getting what we want to happen; it should be about getting what God wants to happen. It's important that we discover what God wants in the Bible and through the prompting of his Holy Spirit – this will help us pray for the things that God wants us to pray for.

Give us the food we need for each day…
God wants us to ask him for things – just like a child would ask his parent for things. But notice how Jesus uses food (most versions say bread) as the example – something essential. When we ask God for things, are we asking him for things we need or things we want?

Forgive us for our sins, just as we have forgiven those who sinned against us…
When we pray we should confess our sins to God, asking and receiving his forgiveness. Also notice that prayer isn't just about God doing things, we have to do things as well. God forgives us, so he also expects us to forgive others. We should pray: prayer is one way we can take action, but it's not an opportunity for us to be irresponsible towards the problems we see around us. It's good to pray that God would 'help those experiencing injustice'. But how do you think God might answer those prayers? By telling us to do something about those problems!

And do not cause us to be tempted, but save us from the Evil One…
God rules, but the devil is at work trying to influence us. God is infinitely more powerful than the devil; therefore it makes sense to ask for his protection. Prayer prepares us for the battles we face day-by-day.

What have you included in your prayers over the past few days?

God's top three priorities…	My top three priorities…
1)	1)
2)	2)
3)	3)

Read Matthew 6:9–13. Then, line by line, discuss what we can learn about prayer from the Lord's Prayer. Make a note of one thing you think you need to learn from each line.

Our Father in heaven,

May your name always be kept holy.

May your kingdom come and what you want be done, here on earth as it is in heaven.

Give us the food we need for each day.

Forgive us for our sins, just as we have forgiven those who sinned against us.

And do not cause us to be tempted, but save us from the Evil One.

Questions, thoughts and doodles

Worship

Aim__To explore what worship is really about.

__Leaders' Introduction

The word worship will conjure up a wide variety of thoughts and feelings for different people. For some people it will mean a particular form of service, maybe an 'act of worship' following a set liturgy. For other people, possibly many young people, it will mean a particular event where there is lots of singing.

In this session we are exploring just two verses from the book of Romans that tell us that worship is about much more than just a service or singing. True worship is about our whole lives. It's quite probable that you are very familiar with the verses found in Romans 12:1–2, but read them again...now!

These verses begin with the word 'so'; other versions, such as the NIV, begin with the word 'therefore'. This is always an important clue that what follows is linked and is a result of what's been said before. Up to this point the book of Romans has provided us with an overview of the gospel message. It's spoken about how sinful we are and has explained what Christ has achieved for us. There are a lot of deep theological ideas to get our heads around in the first 11 chapters of Romans! Then, from chapter 12 onwards, Paul really begins to help us consider how we should respond. Since God has shown us great mercy...

'...I beg you to offer your lives as a living sacrifice to him. Your offering must be only for God and pleasing to him, which is the spiritual way for you to worship.' (Romans 12:1)

It's difficult for us to grasp at the beginning of the 21st century, just how odd and striking it must have been for the first hearers of this letter to read the words 'living' and 'sacrifice' one after the other. Sacrifices were all about death, killing animals, and now we are told to live as living sacrifices. Sacrifices have always been an integral part of worship (and not only for the Jews), so the imagery here, especially given the previous 11 chapters of Romans, is extremely vivid. No longer do we need to sacrifice animals in order for our

sins to be dealt with. Christ has made the forgiveness of sins possible by his once-and-for-all sacrifice on the cross. An amazing opportunity has opened up for us because of Christ's sacrifice on the cross, meaning that we can sacrifice our old, sinful lives, and live new transformed lives, through his power, as living sacrifices.

We no longer have to bring animals to God; instead he wants us to bring our lives. He wants us to worship him by living lives that please him. Other versions use the word 'body'. This too would have shocked many of the initial hearers of the letter. The popular view at the time was that the mind was good and the body was evil. So here Paul is saying that God wants you to bring your body, your physical lives – because that can form part of your spiritual worship. It's not just the mind which should be engaged in spiritual activities, but your whole body, your whole lives. We need to stop separating spirituality from other areas of our lives – it's all interconnected.

This is evidenced further in the next verse, which brings our thinking (in other versions our minds) into the picture, again proving how our worship is about everything we are – how we outwardly live our lives (with our bodies) and how we internally think (with our minds).

This session is not about belittling the importance of sung worship, but it is about communicating how much more there is to worship than what takes place on a Sunday.

__Begin

Idea 1

__Title: Worship music quiz
__Why: A fun way to start the session
__With: Music quiz from www.scriptureunion.org.uk/substance, the means to play it, a prize and some song books

> *Download* the music quiz from **www.scriptureunion.org.uk/substance**. It plays extracts from a wide variety of old and modern hymns and songs. Divide the group into teams, play the music and see if they know the song titles. Give them a bonus point if they know the author!
> Have a selection of song books on hand and/or access to the Internet and get everyone to choose their favourite worship song. Ask them to explain to the group why it's their favourite.
> Get the group to discuss with one another why so many people find music and singing songs such a good way of expressing their worship to God.
> Conclude by explaining that in this session we are going to explore that although singing songs is a great way of worshiping God it is not the only way and worship is about so much more than singing songs.

Idea 2

__Title: What do you think?
__Why: To get the young people considering what they think about worship
__With: Two signs and the means to attach them to the wall

> This activity will give the young people in your group an opportunity to express their opinion about various statements. Have a sign at one end of the room that says, 'I totally agree' and one at the other end that says, 'Er… no'. Make sure you clear away any furniture or other obstacles between the two signs!
> Read out each of the statements below in turn and ask the young people to place themselves along the imaginary line between the two signs depending on how strongly they agree or disagree with the statement. You may like to add some of your own statements to this list.
___A good worship session involves loads of singing
___I think worship should be a formal and reverent affair
___I don't really worship God other than in church on a Sunday
___I don't need to go to church to worship God
___I like many different styles of worship

Idea 3

__Title: What is worship?
__Why: To consider what worship is and isn't
__With: Resource page 78, animation file and the means to show it

Get a large sheet of paper, preferably one you can attach to the wall, and write 'Worship is…' in large letters in the middle of it. Give everyone in the group a pen and get them to write down a few words or a sentence explaining what they think worship is.
> Get the group to discuss, in twos or threes, what's been written, before showing them the animation file for this session that can be *downloaded* from **www.scriptureunion.org.uk/substance**. Then ask the group whether they think it is possible for the same act to be carried out with different attitiudes – one being worshipful, the other not. Spend some time exploring how they would describe a 'worshipful' and 'non-worshipful' attitude.
> Photocopy resource page 78 and give a copy to each person in the group (it contains a variety of quotes defining worship.) In twos or threes encourage them to discuss the quotes they most like and the reasons for this. If it's possible for the young people to access the Internet you might like to encourage them to find some quotes about worship for themselves.

__Explore

Idea 1

__Title: Worship for Dummies
__Why: To explore what true
worship is really about
__With: Depends how creative
you'd like to be

> By this stage in the session the young people will already have been thinking a lot about what worship is and isn't. The aim of this idea is for them to think about how they would explain what worship is to other people. Hopefully, by doing this, they'll gain a better understanding for themselves.
> Try to bring in a selection of the 'For dummies' books, or if Internet access is possible show your group the website **www. dummies.com**. Whatever is possible explain the ethos behind the series. As their website says, '*For Dummies books use a light-hearted approach, a down-to-earth style, and even cartoons and humorous icons to dispel fears and inspire confidence. Light-hearted but not lightweight, **For Dummies** books are the perfect survival guide for anyone who finds themselves in difficult situations.*'
> Explain that in groups of about four people you want them to create a '*For Dummies*' style guide to worship. They are to use Romans 12:1–2 as their basis and are to explore as many possible ways of worshipping God as they can. Get them to consider why we should worship and how we should worship. Encourage them to think about attitude as well as practice.
> There are numerous ways

they could present their guides. You could simply get them to come up with notes as to what each chapter would include. '*For Dummies*' guides often include cartoons, so you could get them to draw a series of cartoons that illustrate what they want to communicate. Alternatively, if you have access to laptop computers you could get each group to create a PowerPoint 'Worship for Dummies' guide. You may be able to think of a different way this could be done.
> Whichever way you choose, make sure there is enough time for each group to talk though their 'Worship for Dummies' guide with the rest of the group.

Idea 2

__Title: Living Sacrifices
__Why: To discover what we
can learn about worship from
Romans 12:1–2
__With: Journal page 63

> Use the Journal page, the introductory leaders' notes and the following ideas to explore Romans 12:1–2.
> Ask a volunteer to read Romans 12:1–2. Draw their attention to the fact that the verse starts with, 'So'. In pairs get them to flick through Romans 1–11 and summarise the main themes.
> Using some reference books, the Internet, or the **downloadable** factsheet available from **www.scriptureunion.org.uk/ substance**, get the young people to find out what the initial hearers would have thought about when they heard the word 'sacrifice'.
> Suggest to them that the

phrase 'living sacrifice' is therefore a little odd! Ask them to discuss what they think it means. Prompt the discussion with your own thoughts and those provided in the leaders' introduction.
> In smaller groups, ask the young people to discuss how they can live their 'whole lives as an act of worship'. If you want to discuss this at greater length, go to Idea 3.
> Read verse 2 again to refresh their memories. Then discuss the following questions:
__In what ways can we easily be shaped by the world?
__How does being a Christian involve a new way of thinking?
__What has this got to do with worship?

Idea 3

__Title: Whole life worship
__Why: To realise that worship
is about so much more than
singing songs on a Sunday

> If this is the only idea you are using from the Explore section read Romans 12:1–2 with your group and explain that knowing what's been said in Romans 1–11 should provide us with a real motivation to worship God. Explain how we're going to spend some time thinking about why and how we should worship God with our whole lives, but before we do that we're going to do an activity to illustrate the point.
> Get a few young people, in turn, to talk about something they are really passionate about. However, before they begin to talk, tie their hands behind their backs and make them sit

completely still on a chair – they cannot move anything except their mouth. Once a few young people have had a turn, repeat this activity, but this time they are not restricted in any way. This should illustrate that when you are passionate about something, it's very hard to communicate to others about it, if you don't have the use of your whole body. We communicate a lot of passion through arm and head movements! If we are passionate about God, we surely can't just express that with our mouths on Sunday – we are going to want to express it with our whole lives, throughout the whole week.
> Spend some time making a long list of all the possible ways you could worship God during your week. You may like to do it creatively, for example, going through the alphabet and coming up with one idea for each letter.

__Respond

Idea 1

__Title: Worship this week
__Why: To understand that everything can be done as an act of worship

> Romans 12:1–2 shows us that the spiritual, the physical (what we do) and the mental (what we think) are all connected. Too often we compartmentalise the spiritual. Hopefully, this session has illustrated that they are all linked. Summarise this idea to your group.
> Get your group to make a list of ten things they are going to be doing this week.
> Read Colossians 3:17 and explain that we should do everything, literally everything, in a way that honours God, because this is what it means to worship God with our whole lives.
> Encourage everyone either individually or together to think/ discuss how the ten things they have written down can be done in a way that honours God.
> Conclude by praying for one another.

Idea 2

__Title: Transformed Lives
__Why: To consider our response to God's grace
__With: Some background music and the means to play it

> Put some gentle music on in the background, encourage people to get comfortable, and then read the following story from Victor Hugo's *Les Miserables*.

A man named Jean Valjean is sentenced to 19 years of hard labour for the crime of stealing some bread. Gradually over time Valjean hardened into a tough convict. Eventually he earned his release, but no one would provide lodging for such a person. Eventually he came across a kind bishop who offered him food and shelter.

That night Jean Valjean lay in the most comfortable bed he had ever been in. But as he lay there, he didn't sleep. Instead he waited until the bishop and his sister had drifted off to sleep. The temptation was too great; he went downstairs, rummaged through the cupboards and stole the family silver before creeping off into the darkness.

However, he didn't get very far; the next morning three policemen knocked on the bishop's door, with Valjean in tow. He had been caught and was now waiting to spend the rest of his life in chains. However, when the bishop saw the scene he reacted in a way that no one expected, least of all Valjean.

'So here you are!' the Bishop cried, 'I'm delighted to see you. Had you forgotten that I gave you the candlesticks as well? They are silver like the rest, and worth a good 200 francs. Did you forget to take them?'

Jean Valjean stood there in shock, staring at the old man with an expression no words can convey.

Valjean was no thief, the bishop assured the policemen; this silver was my gift to him.

When the police withdrew, the bishop gave the candlesticks to the trembling, speechless Valjean and said, 'Do not forget, do not ever forget that you promised me to use the money to make yourself an honest man.'

> And that's exactly what he did; he sold all the silver, except the candlesticks which he kept as a reminder, and lived a transformed life serving others.
> Encourage the group to quietly reflect on this story and think about how they are going to respond to what Christ has done for them.

Idea 3

__Title: Now we'll move into a time of worship...!
__Why: To think about how a 'worship session' in church could communicate what worship is really about

'Now we'll move into a time of worship' is a ridiculous phrase which is said in countless churches every Sunday. Does it mean that what's just happened wasn't worship?!
> Explain this issue to your group and get them to 'design' a 10 or 20 minute 'worship session' that will help those participating in it to grasp what worship is really about.
> Ideally, arrange for your group to actually run their idea at an appropriate service.

Journal
Journal
Journal

Romans 12:1–2 begins with the word 'so'; other versions, such as the NIV, begin with the word 'therefore'. This is always an important clue that what follows is linked and is a result of what's been said before. Up to this point the book of Romans has provided us with an overview of the gospel message. It's spoken about how sinful we are and has explained what Christ has achieved for us. There are a lot of deep theological ideas to get our heads around in the first 11 chapters of Romans! Then, from chapter 12 onwards Paul really begins to help us consider how we should respond. Since God has shown us great mercy...

'...I beg you to offer your lives as a living sacrifice to him. Your offering must be only for God and pleasing to him, which is the spiritual way for you to worship.' (Romans 12:1)

It's difficult for us to grasp at the beginning of the 21st century, just how odd and striking it must have been for the first hearers of this letter to read the words 'living' and 'sacrifice' one after the other. Sacrifices were all about death, killing animals, and now we are told to live as living sacrifices. Sacrifices have always been an integral part of worship (not only for the Jews), so the imagery here, especially given the previous 11 chapters of Romans, is extremely vivid. We no longer need to sacrifice animals in order for our sins to be dealt with. Christ has made the forgiveness of sins possible by his once-and-for-all sacrifice on the cross. An amazing opportunity has opened up for us because of Christ's sacrifice on the cross meaning that we can sacrifice our old, sinful lives, and live new transformed lives, through his power.

We no longer have to bring animals to God; instead he wants us to bring our lives. He wants us to worship him by living lives that please him. Other versions use the word 'body'. This too would have shocked many of the initial hearers of the letter. The popular view at the time was that the mind was good and the body was evil. So here Paul is saying that God wants you to bring your body, your physical lives – because that can form part of your spiritual worship. It's not just the mind which should be engaged in spiritual activities, but your whole body, your whole lives. We need to stop separating spirituality from other areas of our lives – it's all interconnected.

This is evidenced further in the next verse, which brings our thinking (in other versions our minds) into the picture, again proving how our worship is about everything we are – how we outwardly live our lives (with our bodies) and how we internally think (with our minds).

Flick through Romans 1–11 and make a note of the main themes.

When the original hearers of the letter heard the word, 'sacrifice', what would they have associated it with?

What does it mean to be a 'living sacrifice'?

What does 'whole life worship' look like?

In what ways can we easily be shaped by the world?
How does being a Christian involve a new way of thinking?
What has this got to do with worship?

Questions, thoughts and doodles

Church

Aim__To explore what church should be like.

__Leaders' Introduction

The church: many see it as an outdated institution, and all too often it might well appear that way, but actually, the church is one of God's best ideas. As Bill Hybels says, *'The local church is the hope of the world.'*

This session will give you the opportunity to explore what church should really be like. Why is it important? What should it be doing? And how can we play our part?

During this session encourage the young people to see the potential of church – it's an exciting group to be a part of. However, approach this session with care. Many young people really struggle with church, and this session could all too quickly turn into an opportunity to moan and criticise every little thing about the church they belong to. Make sure this does not happen! After all, the church is described as 'the bride of Christ' (1 Corinthians 12), so slating the church is like slating your best friend's boy/girlfriend! That said, no church is perfect, so do give space for the young people to discuss what they find difficult about church. Encourage them to be proactive, to get involved and become part of the solution.

Acts 2:42–47 gives us a fascinating insight into the early church. They were a community who appear to have spent lots of time together. They were really involved in each other's lives.

They spent their time... learning the apostles' teaching. This is about relevant Bible teaching, relating what the Bible says to everyday life, getting to grips with exactly what Jesus has done for us and realising how that should affect our lives.

They spent their time... sharing. Other versions use the word 'fellowship'. They were a community, they built strong friendships with one another and they put the needs of others above their own needs.

They spent their time... breaking bread. They took the Lord's Supper together. In doing so they remembered what Christ achieved through his death and resurrection. This would help ensure that they remained a Christ-centred community.

They spent their time... praying together. As they prayed together they no doubt developed their relationship with God as well as it being a way of supporting one another.

As we continue reading verses 43–46 we discover just how selfless their community was. This session will give you an opportunity to discuss what we need to learn from these verses. Then in verse 47 we read that they were 'liked by all the people'. Can you say that about your church community? Are people attracted to it because of the way you relate to one another and what you stand for? Finally, we read something very exciting. This is a growing community: every day people were being added as more and more people discovered Jesus for themselves.

Wouldn't you just love to be a part of a community like that, who are experiencing those kinds of results?

__Begin

__Title: Church on *The Simpsons*
__Why: To explore what many
  people think church is like
__With: A selection of clips from
  The Simpsons and the means
  to show them

> See if you can get hold of one
or more of these *The Simpson*
episodes. Alternatively you may
know of other episodes that raise
issues surrounding church.
___Homer the Heretic (Season 4)
  00:00 – 08:08
___In Marge We Trust (Season 8)
  00:00 – 03:08
___Faith Off (Season 11) – 10:51
  – 11:38

> Discuss with your group the
picture of church *The Simpsons*
paints. In what way is it similar or
different from their experiences
of church? Get the group to make
a list of words they think their
friends would use to describe
church.

__Title: Designer Church
__Why: To encourage the group
  to begin to think about what
  church should be like

> Divide the group into twos and
threes and ask them to imagine
they have to design a church from
scratch. Get them to write and/
or draw what their church would
be like.
> Keep the instructions and
guidelines to a minimum and just
sit back and see where the young
people go with this task!

> Once they have designed
their church get them to talk to
the rest of the group about it.
Use this, and any discussion it
creates, as the basis for the rest
of the session. You might like to
repeat this activity at the end of
the session to see how they would
revise their plans.

__Title: Healthy Body
__Why: To introduce the idea
  of keeping the body of Christ
  healthy
__With: Quiz on page 79 and/or
  equipment for circuit training
  activities

> Introduce this activity by
explaining that many people
spend lots of time and money
on making their bodies look
good – whether that's by going
to the gym, spending a fortune
on make-up or having cosmetic
surgery. The church is described
as the 'body of Christ'
(1 Corinthians 12), but do we give
the church as much attention as
our bodies? In this session we
will be exploring what a healthy
church is like and what we can do
to ensure our church is healthy.
> Use one of the following
activities to introduce the session.
> **Quiz.** The quiz that can be
found on page 79 illustrates
just how obsessed some people
are about making their own
bodies look good. Conclude by
challenging the group to consider
whether we need to be more
concerned about the 'body of
Christ'.
> **Circuit Training.** If space
allows do some 'circuit training'

activities. (*Download* specific
ideas from **www.scriptureunion.
org.uk/substance**.) Conclude
by explaining that just like it's
important to take care of our
bodies (eg by eating healthily
and keeping fit) we also need to
ensure that the 'body of Christ,
the church, remains healthy.

__Explore

Idea 1

__Title: What makes a church a church?
__Why: To consider what the essential 'ingredients' of church are
__With: Journal page 69, pens and animation file

> Begin by asking the group these ridiculously simple questions:
___What makes a football club a football club?
___What makes a restaurant a restaurant?
___What makes a clothes shop a clothes shop?
___What makes a band a band?

> Then ask them the question (and make notes on a large piece of paper):
___What makes a church a church?

> *Download* and show the group the animation file that accompanies this session. Allow a little time for discussion before moving on.
> Using journal page 69 and the information from the leaders' introduction get them to read the various Bible passages and discuss what they consider are the essential 'ingredients' of a church.
> Conclude by asking the group a variation on the first group of questions (making notes as you feel is appropriate):
___What makes a football club a good football club?
___What makes a restaurant a good restaurant?
___What makes a clothes shop a

good clothes shop?
___What makes a band a good band?
___What makes a church a good church?

Idea 2

__Title: Church – Then and Now
__Why: To consider what we can learn from the early church
__With: If possible a selection of books and Internet access

> Acts 2:42–47 describes a pretty impressive sounding community. However, that was almost 2000 years ago, so in what ways should church today look like it did 2000 years ago and in what ways should it look very different?
> Get the group to read Acts 2:42–47, 1 Corinthians 14:26–40 and ideally the whole of Titus. If possible also provide them with a selection of relevant books (your minister might be able to help here) and Internet access. Ask the group, in twos or threes, to create a summary of what the church was like 2000 years ago.
> Conclude by discussing, either in their small groups or as a whole group, some of the following questions:
___In what ways do you think church should be the same as it was 2000 years ago?
___In what ways do you think church should be different from how it was 2000 years ago?
___Very few churches appear to be literally putting Acts 2:44,45 into practice today. Do you think they should be? Why (not)?
___What key principles can we learn from Acts 2:42–47 and

how should we relate them to our church today?

Idea 3

__Title: Healthy Church
__Why: To explore what a healthy church should look like
__With: Journal page 69

> Explain to the group that they are now 'church consultants/ detectives/analysts' who visit churches to give them a 'health check'.
> Divide the group into twos or threes and ask each group to create a list of ten questions (or indicators) they would use to 'assess' whether a church is healthy or not.
> Encourage them to read the Bible passages found on the journal page as they create their questions. Once they have created their list of questions, get them to share with the wider group why they think each of their questions is important.
> If time allows you may also like to explore the letters to the seven churches that are found in Revelation 2,3 with your group. Ask each group to read one or two of the letters and make a note of the good and bad points mentioned within them. Get them to share their lists with the wider group before discussing what lessons we can learn from these letters.

__Respond

Idea 1

__Title: Get involved
__Why: To encourage the group to participate in church, not just observe
__With: Possibly a board game and a church leader

> Play a game. A board game would probably work well, but make sure it won't take too long. Monopoly would not be a good idea! However, only let half the group play the game, the other half have to watch. Explain that a game is so much more fun if you get to participate in it. Church is the same; it's not something we should observe, it is something we should participate in. Read 1 Corinthians 12:12–31.

> As a group discuss ways you could become more involved in the life of your church. As the leader, make sure you have some ideas up your sleeves! Speak to your church leader and find out in advance some possible ways.

> Alternatively, why not invite your minister or someone from you church leadership team into the final part of your session. It would give the group the opportunity to have an honest conversation with them about the church and discuss how they could become more involved. Make sure it's a two-way conversation! Ensure that the leader both encourages and challenges the young people and that the group both encourage and challenge the leader.

Idea 2

__Title: Pray for the church
__Why: To stress the importance of praying for the church
__With: Depends on how creative you want to be!

> The aim of this idea is to get the group to pray for the church – be as creative as possible. Here are a few ideas to get you started:
> Pray for your church, the churches in your town and the worldwide church (maybe you could focus on the persecuted church). Set up three different stations around the room with information and pointers for prayer.
> Invite a few people from your church who lead a certain aspect of ministry (for example, children's worker, caretaker, pastoral worker). If there are aspects of your church's life that your group probably don't know much about, try especially hard to get representatives to the session. Get each person to talk about their area of ministry for a couple of minutes. (Give them clear direction as to exactly what you want from them in advance.) Then invite the young people to pray for them and their ministry.
> If your group meet in the church building (and there are not too many other groups meeting at the same time!) walk around the building, explaining as you go what activities take place where. Pause in each location to pray for these activities.

Idea 3

__Title: Health Plan
__Why: To come up with a 'health plan' for your group

> Your group is an important part of your church. Therefore the health of your group will have an impact on the health of the church. The aim of this idea is to apply the principles we've explored during this session directly to your group.
> Divide the young people into smaller groups and ask them to discuss what they want your group to look like in one year's time. Ask them to think about what needs to happen between now and then to achieve that.
> Conclude by asking them to consider everything we've learnt in this session to come up with a 'ten-point health plan' for the group.

Journal
__Journal
Journal
Journal

Acts 2:42-47 gives us a fascinating insight into the early church. They were a community who appear to have spent lots of time together. They were really involved in each other's lives.

They spent their time... learning the apostles' teaching. This is about relevant Bible teaching, relating what the Bible says to everyday life, getting to grips with exactly what Jesus has done for us and realising how that should affect our lives.

They spent their time... sharing. Other versions use the word 'fellowship'. They were a community, they built strong friendships with one another and they put the needs of others above their own needs.

They spent their time... breaking bread. They took the Lord's Supper together. In doing so they remembered what Christ achieved through his death and resurrection. This would help ensure that they remained a Christ-centred community.

They spent their time... praying together. As they prayed together they no doubt developed their relationship with God as well as it being a way of supporting one another.

As we continue reading verse 43-46 we discover just how selfless their community was. Then in verse 47 we read that they were 'liked by all the people'. Can you say that about your church community? Are people attracted to it because of the way you relate to one another and what you stand for? Finally we read something very exciting. This is a growing community: every day people were being added as more and more people discovered Jesus for themselves.

Wouldn't you just love to be a part of a community like that, who are experiencing those kinds of results?

What makes a football club a football club?

What makes a restaurant a restaurant?

What makes a clothes shop a clothes shop?

What makes a band a band?

What makes a church a church?

Read the following Bible passages and create a 'recipe' for a good church. Focus on the essential 'ingredients'.

- Acts 2:42-47
- Romans 12:4-5
- Ephesians 2:19-22
- Ephesians 4:11-17
- 1 Peter 2:5
- Hebrews 10:24-25

What makes a football club a **good** football club?

What makes a restaurant a **good** restaurant?

What makes a clothes shop and **good** clothes shop?

What makes a band a **good** band?

What makes a church a good church?

Questions, thoughts and doodles

Resources

__Inventors

Joseph Lister
England
(1867)

Alfred Nobel
Sweden
(1867)

Louis S. Lenormand
France
(1783)

Lazlo Biró
Argentina
(1944)

King C. Gillette
US
(1901)

Samuel Colt
US
(1835)

Walter Hunt
US
(1849)

Isaac Singer
US
(1851)

Valdemar Poulsen
Denmark
(1899)

Benjamin Holt
US
(1900)

W.L. Judson
US
(1891)

Charles Goodyear
US
(1839)

Henry Ford
US
(1913)

Martin Schadt Wolfgang Helfrich
Switzerland
(1970)

Edwin Budding John Ferrabee
England
(1830–1831)

Sir Frank Whittle
England
Hans von Ohain
Germany
(1936)

Wallace H. Carothers
US
(1935)

Elisha G. Otis
US
(1852)

Louis Braille
France
(1829)

Joseph and Jacques Montgolfier
France
(1783)

__Inventions

Antiseptic	Dynamite	Parachute	Ball point pen
Safety razor	Revolver	Safety pin	Continuous-stitch sewing machine
Tape recorder	Tractor	Zip	Rubber
Moving assembly line	Liquid crystal display	Lawn mower	Jet propulsion engine
Nylon	Passenger elevator	Braille	Hot air balloon

ANSWERS: Antiseptic – Joseph Lister, dynamite – Alfred Nobel, parachute – Louis S. Lenormand, ball point pen – Lazlo Biró, safety razor – King Gillette, revolver – Samuel Colt, safety pin – Walter Hunt, continuous-stitch sewing machine – Isaac Singer, tape recorder – Valdemar Poulsen, tractor – Benjamin Holt, zip – W.L. Judson, rubber – Charles Goodyear, moving assembly line – Henry Ford, liquid crystal display – Martin Schadt and Wolfgang Helfrich, lawn mower – Edwin Budding and John Ferrabee, jet propulsion engine – Sir Frank Whittle and Hans von Ohain, nylon – Wallace H. Carothers, passenger elevator – Elisha G. Otis, braille – Louis Braille, hot air balloon – Joseph and Jacques Montgolfier.

__Amazing facts quiz

1)	A human being blinks over 10,000 times a year.	**TRUE**
2)	A giraffe can clean its ears with its 21-inch tongue.	**TRUE**
3)	The average person walks the equivalent of six times around the world in a lifetime.	**FALSE** (two times)
4)	Experts estimate that there might be approximately 2 million different species of insects in the world.	**FALSE** (10 million)
5)	Your heart will beat around 40,000,000 times a year.	**TRUE**
6)	The world's largest mammal, the blue whale, weighs 50 tons at birth. Fully grown, it weighs as much as 150 tons.	**TRUE**
7)	50,000 of the cells in your body will die and be replaced with new cells, all while you have been reading this sentence!	**TRUE**
8)	A hippopotamus can run faster than a man.	**TRUE**
9)	The eye of a human can distinguish 2000 shades of grey.	**FALSE** (500)
10)	The average human has about 5,000 taste buds.	**FALSE** (10,000)
11)	A fully grown adult has 206 bones, a newborn baby has 250.	**FALSE** (a newborn baby has 350)
12)	If you were to put all your blood vessels in a long line you could stretch them round the world 2.5 times.	**TRUE**
13)	It is estimated that our digestive system handles about 5 tonnes of food in our lifetime.	**FALSE** (50 tonnes)
14)	A sneeze can generate a wind of up to 100 miles per hour.	**TRUE**
15)	Cell by cell, half a child's entire skeleton is replaced in one year.	**TRUE**

__A typical day

Before school/college/work

During school/college/work

After school/college work

During the night

___The exile: they should have seen it coming!

It's often said that people are predictable – the Israelites certainly were! The pages of the Old Testament contain a pattern which is repeated time and time again. 1) God does something amazing... 2) The people praise him and follow him... 3) They forget about him... 4) Things begin to go wrong for them... 5) They cry out and ask for his help... 6) He helps them by doing something amazing... 7) The pattern continues...!

The people of Israel were frequently warned about the exile. God made it clear to them that if they didn't obey him he would throw them out of the Promised Land. But it appears they didn't listen. Here's a quick overview of the rise and fall of the nation of Israel.

Abraham

God makes some massive promises to Abram (his name was later changed to Abraham). He promised to make his descendants into a nation. They were to follow God and reveal him to the whole world. Part of the promise included being given land. Abraham and his family have their ups and downs, but although they make some big mistakes they usually do their best to follow God. [Genesis 12:1–9]

Egypt

Joseph ended up in Egypt, as did his brothers to avoid the famine. They settled down and things went well for them. However, after 400 years there were rather a lot of them, and Pharaoh had forgotten how the Israelites came to be in Egypt in the first place. The Israelites were forced into slavery and things became very bad for them. However, God heard their cries and sent Moses. [Exodus 1:1–14, 2:23–25, 3:7–10]

Exodus

Moses led the Israelites out of Egypt on an epic journey to the Promised Land – the land promised to Abraham many years ago. Things started off well [Exodus 12,13], then they got really bad [Exodus 32]. There were moments when things seemed to go OK, but generally things were pretty bad [Numbers 14]. The people of Israel seemed to be very good at complaining and forgetting what God had done for them.

Promised Land

Because of their disobedience in the desert it took the Israelites many more years than necessary to enter the Promised Land. However, they eventually arrived and God helped them take control of the land – have a look at the book of Joshua to find out more. Before Joshua died (he had taken over from Moses as their leader) he warned the people that they must continue to obey God if they wanted to go forwards; disobedience would lead to them being thrown out of the Promised Land. [Joshua 23:12–13]

Judges

During the time of Joshua the people (on the whole!) obeyed God [Judges 2:7], but after he had died things began to slip [Judges 2:10–14]. Then, throughout the book of Judges we see 'the pattern' extremely clearly. Each time the Israelites get themselves in a mess God sends a 'Judge' to sort them out. Things go well for a while, then the people forget about God and things go badly again. Browse through the book of Judges to see 'the pattern' in action.

Kings

In the end the Israelites decided they wanted a king like the other nations (up to then they had been content with God as their king). First there was Saul, who disobeyed God rather a lot [1 Samuel 15:22–26]. Then there was David, who despite making some very big mistakes was a pretty good king [2 Samuel 7:18–29]. Next there was Solomon who started well [1 Kings 4:29–34] but ended badly [1 Kings 11]. From then on it was a bit 'hit and miss'. Unfortunately there appeared to be more 'misses' than 'hits'! There were good kings that would bring the people back to God [like Josiah – 2 Kings 23:25 and Hezekiah – 2 Kings 18:5–8] and bad kings that would lead the people away from God [like Jeroboam and Nadab – 1 Kings 15:25,26]. Civil war broke out and the nation of Israel was divided into two – a northern kingdom (Israel) and a southern kingdom (Judah). Prophets were sent warning the people of God's judgement and urging them to turn back to God. Take a look at the books of Hosea, Joel, Micah and Jeremiah.

Exile

Eventually enough was enough, God had given his people plenty of warnings [Jeremiah 7:3,7,14], but they failed to act. The northern nation of Israel was invaded from the north by the Assyrians in 722BC [2 Kings 17]. The cities were destroyed and the people were taken captive – never to be heard of again. The southern nation of Judah was captured by the Babylonians in 586BC [2 Kings 25]. Jerusalem was destroyed and all the young men (for example Daniel) and women were taken to Babylon as prisoners [Daniel 1].

__Problem page

It all started to go a bit wrong last week when my best friend said something really horrible to me. It really hurt me. Then, if that wasn't bad enough, I discovered that my best friend has also been saying some pretty nasty things about me behind my back to my other friends. I'm really not sure why all this is happening and I don't know what I should do.

I appear to be short of money at the moment. And that's a real problem! My friend has just bought a new computer and has some fantastic games. I desperately need to upgrade mine, and I need some decent games as well. Then there's that new CD; I really need to buy it before anyone else does. Then, my clothes – well, they are getting a bit old now, and I saw this really nice coat in a magazine last week – I just have to have it. But, I need more money! And my parents won't give me any more, it's just not fair! What do you think I should do?

I'm taking my A levels at the end of this year and I just don't know what to do next. Do I take a gap year, go to uni or get a job? I need to make a decision quickly, but I don't want to make the wrong one, because what I decide to do will dramatically change the rest of my life. How on earth should I go about making such a big decision? What happens if I do the wrong thing?

My friend is very unhappy at the moment. She keeps talking to me about all the problems she faces. She's managed to get herself into a right mess. Personally, I think it's her own fault; she's made some bad decisions. She's been horrible to her parents, started taking drugs, always getting drunk and now she's sleeping around quite a bit. What should I do?

__Maze

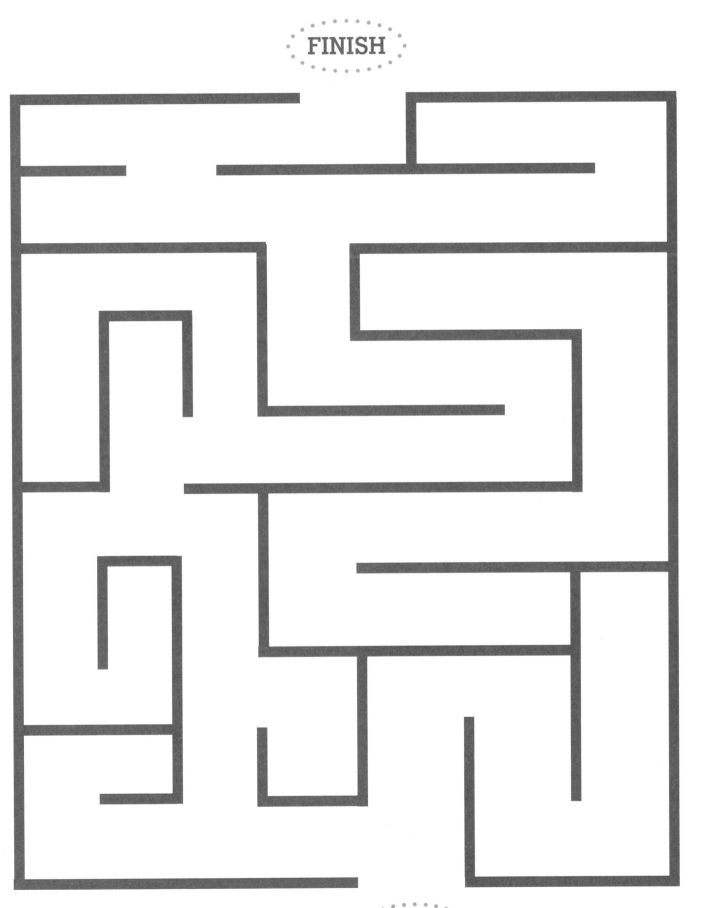

__Worship quotes

'Worship is God's enjoyment of us, and our enjoyment of Him.'
(Graham Kendrick)

'Worship is to feel in the heart, and to express in some appropriate manner, a humbling but delightful sense of admiring awe and astonished wonder.' *(A.W. Tozer)*

'Worship is about intimacy with God. Worship is the act of freely giving love to God (it forms and informs every activity of the Christian's life). Worship is also an expression of awe, submission and respect towards God' *(John Wimber)*

'Worship is to quicken the conscience by the holiness of God, to feed the mind with the truth of God, to purge the imagination by the beauty of God, to devote the will to the purpose of God.' *(William Temple – a former Archbishop of Canterbury)*

'Worship is a participation sport in a spectator culture.' *(Louie Giglio)*

'A person will worship something, have no doubt about that. We may think our tribute is paid in secret in the dark recesses of our hearts, but it will out. That which dominates our imaginations and our thoughts will determine our lives, and our character. Therefore, it behoves us to be careful what we worship, for what we are worshipping we are becoming." *(Ralph Waldo)*

'An authentic life is the most personal form of worship. Everyday life has become my prayer.' *(Sarah Ban Breathnach)*

'Why did men worship in churches, locking themselves away in the dark, when the world lay beyond its doors in all its real glory?' *(Charles de Lint)*

__Quiz

1)   How much money is it estimated that Britons will spend on Cosmetic surgery in 2008?

a) £100 million   *b) £1 billion*   c) £10 billion

2)   How much does the average British woman spend on her hair during her lifetime?

a) £18,000   b) £23,000   *c) £28,000*

3)   The average Brit spends how much money in their lifetime on clothes they never wear?

a) £2,000   b) £4,000   *c) £6,000*

4)   How much money does the average woman spend on make-up during her lifetime?

a) £8,500   b) £12,500   c) £15,500

5)   How much money does the average British man spend on his hair each year?

a) £219   b) £319   c) £419

6)   On average, how much do British women spend on clothes each year?

a) £800   *b) £1,800*   c) £2,800

7)   How much did British men (combined) spend on grooming products in 2007?

a) £427 million   b) £627 million   *c) £827 million*

SUbstance Volume 2

__Contents

Volume 2

__Module

KINGDOM:guide

The kingdom of God is a big ideal It's an idea that runs throughout the entire Bible. The Old Testament provides us glimpses of the kingdom, Jesus came to establish the kingdom, the church should be advancing the kingdom and Christ's return will usher in the kingdom in all its perfect fullness. This module aims to help young people grasp this kingdom idea and, in the process, transform their understanding of Christianity.

__Module

KINGDOM:living

When you visit a foreign country you will often read a guidebook that tells you what to expect. The guidebook explains the culture, the customs and the rules of the country you are visiting. This module explores the 'Sermon on the Mount', a guidebook to the 'kingdom of God' which explains how we are meant to live as residents in God's kingdom.

ANSWERS TO PAGE 51

1) Revelation 1:12–15
2) Deuteronomy 18:9,10
3) Matthew 13:44
4) Proverbs 14:30

c) Apocalyptic
d) Law
a) Parables
g) Wise sayings

5) Joshua 1:1,2
6) Philippians 4:2–4
7) Amos 1:6,7
8) Psalm 98:8,9

e) History
b) Letters
h) Prophecy
f) Song